# HOW TO BUILD
# YOUR DREAM CABIN
# IN THE WOODS

# Books by J. Wayne Fears

*The Complete Book of Canoe Camping*
*Turkey Guide*
*The Sportsman's Guide to Swamp Camping*
*Trout Fishing the Southern Appalachians*
*The Canoer's Bible* – co-author
*Cooking the Wild Harvest*
*The Muzzleloading Hunters Handbook*
*The Wild Turkey Book*
*The Field & Stream Wilderness Cooking Handbook*
*Successful Turkey Hunting*
*Hunting Whitetails Successfully*
*Scrape Hunting From A to Z*
*Hunting North America's Big Bears*
*The Complete Book of Outdoor Survival*

# HOW TO BUILD YOUR DREAM CABIN IN THE WOODS

*The Ultimate Guide to Building and Maintaining a Backcountry Getaway*

J. Wayne Fears

SKYHORSE PUBLISHING

Skyhorse Publishing books may be purchased in bulk at special discounts for sales promotion, corporate gifts, fund-raising, or educational purposes. Special editions can also be created to specifications. For details, contact the Special Sales Department, Skyhorse Publishing, 307 West 36th Street, 11th Floor, New York, NY 10018 or info@skyhorsepublishing.com.

Skyhorse® and Skyhorse Publishing® are registered trademarks of Skyhorse Publishing, Inc.®, a Delaware corporation.

www.skyhorsepublishing.com

10 9 8 7 6 5 4 3 2 1

Library of Congress Cataloging-in-Publication Data is available on file.

ISBN: 978-1-62914-653-9

Printed in China

*Dedicated to my daughter*
*Carla Fears Schmit*
*You are my hero*

# Contents

CHAPTER

# 1

# The Dream—A Cabin
# in the Woods

Imagine, if you will, a small cabin tucked away in a forest. It is located on a small knoll just above a rushing creek. The cabin, lit by the warm glow of a kerosene lamp, is not large, just one room with a wood-burning stove in one corner, bunk beds in another. In the third corner is a simple kitchen with a sink, cabinet, and camp stove. In the middle of the room is a table, covered with a cheerful oilcloth tablecloth surrounded by four chairs. A small bookcase along one wall holds the books you have always wished you had time to read, and a fly rod hangs over the door. The patter of rain on the metal roof blending with the crackle of a burning log in the stove is all it takes to make you relax and drift towards a peaceful sleep.

Outside the cabin is a woodshed filled with split logs, the results of honest work from the past summer, guaranteeing warm visits here. On a small rise to one side of the cabin is a cheerful outhouse; clean, bright, and critter proof. On the other side is a fire pit, an extension of the cabin and the favorite gathering place of close friends and family. Here many meals have been prepared in Dutch ovens, reflector ovens and on hooks hanging above the open fire.

This cabin is all yours to use on those weekends and vacations when the most valuable thing you can do is to escape the real world and get back to a place where living is simple and truly peaceful. Your cabin is a place where you can get to know your spouse, your children, perhaps grandchildren, or, most important, yourself. It is a place to launch grand adventures such as trying to outsmart that ten-point buck you have seen down by the apple orchard, or renewing your efforts to catch that big brown trout in the deep hole where the creek runs under the bridge you built two summers ago. Perhaps the adventure will be exploring, painting, photography, canoeing, or

1

seeing if you can catch a glimpse of that barred owl you hear at night, a great addition to your birding life list. Whatever your reason, your dream cabin is a place where you have peace and quiet to recharge the human spirit.

## YOU ARE NOT THE FIRST TO DREAM

I don't think I have ever met a person that liked the outdoors that didn't want a dream cabin in the woods. Such writers as Anne LaBastille, Russell Annabel, Robert Service, and Jack London have fostered the romantic appeal of a small, simple cabin nestled in a remote hideaway. Henry David Thoreau lived and worked in his one-room cabin on Walden Pond; Aldo Leopold loved the cabin he loved called "The Shack". Well known bow hunter and outdoor writer Fred Bear had a camp called Grouse Haven; *Outdoor Life* magazine field editor Charlie Elliott had a cabin in a place called Beech Bottoms; Horace Kephart had a cabin on Hazel Creek in the Southern Great Smoky Mountains; Bradford Angier had a cabin on the Peace River in British Columbia; and George W. Sears, who wrote under the name

Almost every outdoorsman has dreamed of a small cabin located deep in the woods such as this Alaskan trapper's-style cabin located near Fairbanks.

Photo by JWF

Nessmuk, had several Adirondack shelters he called home in the backcountry. The list could go on and on, but the point is a cabin in the woods has been the dream, and a part of the life, of many who love the outdoors.

My dream of a cabin in the woods came at an early age. I may have been in junior high school when I started reading Jack London and his books about the far North. His characters lived in log cabins, and I could see myself in such a cabin.

One day I borrowed a book from the school library titled *Cache Lake Country,* by John Rowlands. This book took cabin living to the next level, describing how the author built his one-room cabin in the Canadian wilderness and detailing his daily life for a full year. It was a grand adventure, and I dreamed of someday having my own cabin in the woods.

Since those early days, I have seen my dream come true many times. Not only have I built my own cabins in the woods, but also have stayed in other backcountry cabins throughout the world, each of which not only

Renowned outdoor writer Horace Kephart, inside his cabin on Hazel Creek deep in the Great Smoky Mountains.

Photo by National Park Service

gave me shelter but taught me something of the owner. Wilderness cabins are like fingerprints; no two are exactly alike. Each cabin is the dream of its builder and each is individual, as the builder puts something of himself into its design and building. It is in this spirit of expressing your own thoughts of cabin design, building, and living, that this book was written.

My cabins have been most rewarding not just as a place for my family and friends to relax and enjoy outdoor adventures, but each has become an ongoing hobby; as an Alaskan friend once told me, a cabin is a "work in progress".

We are always seeing something to add, improve, or develop in or around our cabin. I think a cabin should never be finished, as there would be little fun. Just when we think it is finished, we see something to improve and our hobby continues. As Conrad Meinecke stated in his classic cabin book *Your Cabin In the Woods,* published in 1945, "Your cabin-in-the-woods should always present enough challenge to keep you constantly adding to its loveliness. In this way after each visit you will return to your city life rested, stronger, revived."

When you build your own cabin, you will find that a cabin takes on its own personality. I always enjoy the comments of first-time visitors to the cabin, who'll say, "It's like coming home" or "It's so peaceful." After they have stayed there a few days and must leave, I hear them say, "Goodbye little cabin, I hope to see you again soon." Our cabin has a warm and inviting personality that quickly puts one at ease. Yours, too, will have its unique qualities that you alone can bring.

It is my strong belief that everyone who wants a cabin in the woods should strive to realize that dream. It is obtainable for most, even if we are of modest means. One of the reasons I wrote this book is to encourage you not to wait too long. Live your dream while you can. You won't be sorry.

## THE PURPOSE OF THIS BOOK

This book is not going to make you a better carpenter, plumber, or rock mason. It is not going to take you step-by-step through the steps of laying logs or framing, or teach you construction skills. There are lots of books available on those subjects that do a much better job than I ever could. Many of these books are listed in the appendix of this book, and I suggest you read and study them.

The purpose of this book is to encourage you to realize your dream and to help you plan it, eliminating the pitfalls. The planning of a cabin is as

Cabin planning dates back to the earliest beginnings of this country, and many of the designs have changed little.                                    Photo by JWF

much fun as the building of it. Since it is your dream cabin, you should do as much of the construction as you can. This book will give you many cabin-type design options to consider, from the simple Adirondack shelter to the multi-bedroom modern cabin. We will discuss finding land, picking a site, planning and outfitting the cabin, and tips to make cabin living fun. The backcountry cabin need not be expensive, and I will show you how to cut costs.

In this book, I will stress simplicity. Most of the book is geared toward building a cabin in a remote area where public utilities are not an option nor are they wanted. There is a special pride of ownership associated with a cabin that is totally self-sufficient. The totally self-sufficient cabin with no water pipes to freeze and no electrical lines to go out in storms, teaches the users a simple way of life that is cozy and peaceful, and is a lot less expensive. In addition, if the world should go to hell in a handbasket, for a short period or a long haul, be it a manmade or natural crisis, the self-sufficient cabin will be worth its weight in gold. We leave our cabin fully stocked and ready to live in, except for perishables. All we have to do is show up with milk, bread, and ice and begin having fun living in the woods. It sure makes planning and packing for a long weekend getaway quick and easy.

If well built, old-time cabins such as this one in New Mexico will far outlast their builders.

Photo by JWF

We had all this in mind when developing our thoughts regarding Cross Creek Hollow, our dream cabin in the woods. It was important to know what we wanted to accomplish both personally and professionally.

Enough talking about what we are going to do; let's get down to the planning of your future cabin and start you on the path to spending weekends and vacations in your cabin. It will become your favorite place to get away from it all. Leaving your cabin will be difficult every time you must go back to the working world. However, one of the good things about having your own cabin tucked away in the woods is that you always know it's there, and you can dream of the next trip, even if you are at work.

CHAPTER

## 2

# Selecting a Site

F inding the perfect location for your cabin in the woods can be a fun adventure or it can be a nightmare. It is the most important step in building a cabin, as the best cabin ever built, on the wrong site, can be nothing but trouble and expense. If you already own the land where you want to build your cabin, or you can use family land, then you can skip the first part of this chapter.

First, we need to determine what "in the woods" means to you. "The woods" means different things to different people. To some it may be a remote canyon in a desert; to others it may be the farm woodlot. Recently I visited one of the best-designed one-room cabins I have ever seen. There are trappers in the far north who would give their eyeteeth for a cabin like this one. It wasn't set in the far North, however; it was in a large city in Florida. In fact, the lady who designed the trapper-style cabin isn't interested in the backcountry. She lives on a one-acre lot with a wooded corner where she sought solitude. Here she built the cabin as a place she could spend her midday hours reading, listening to classical music, and taking a nap. She doesn't spend nights there, but she does use it as a guest cottage, and tells me her guests love it. This is her dream cabin in the woods.

Before you begin the all-important search for your cabin site, write down a description of the setting that you mentally visualize your cabin occupying, on a large lake, on a small pond, on the banks of a rushing stream, in a valley or desert canyon, on a wooded hill with mountain views, or in the heart of big game country. Take your time and write a detailed description that includes your desired climate, surroundings, how modern or self-sufficient you want your cabin, and what recreational pursuits you are interested in. This will help you later in your search for land.

Once you have your desires for a cabin setting written down, next determine how much land you will want. Most people start out wanting large tracts

"In the woods" means different things to different people. This dream cabin sits on the edge of a modern city in Alaska.                    Photo by JWF

of land until they see the price of land. Be realistic in what you can spend on land, now and in the future. There will be annual taxes and maintenance costs from now on. If hunting, fishing, birding, or hiking is what you want land for, remember you can locate your cabin on a small tract of land near or adjacent to public lands or private lands with public access, where these activities can be enjoyed. If you want solitude, it doesn't take a huge wilderness area to find solitude. As the lady in Florida proved, you can find solitude on small tracts.

Before you begin looking for specific parcels, you need to set up a budget for either buying or leasing land. At this point, you must be very realistic with yourself. Only you know how much you can spend on land. Don't forget there will be other costs associated with land acquisition in addition to the cost of the land itself. There will be travel costs to look at potential sites, long distance phone calls, attorney fees, possibly appraisal, survey, and closing costs. If you get a long-term lease on a site, many of these costs will be eliminated, but there may be additional up-front costs such as insurance and the first year's lease payment. Knowing realistically what you have to spend on the cabin project will be a great help in knowing how much land to look for and the size cabin you can expect to build.

## SOLITUDE, IS IT FOR YOU?

Back to the subject of solitude, let's discuss whether solitude is really what you want. I have known of more backcountry cabins being sold, soon after being built, due to too much solitude rather than too little. Most of us who live in the United States today really do not know what solitude is. We are rarely in a room alone for a long period of time, much less alone in a cabin for a long weekend. Until you have really tried living in a solitary situation for a period of time and have proven to yourself that you like it, don't hold out for a cabin on a lonely island or at the end of a road miles from the nearest neighbor. Perhaps you would prefer some privacy, giving you enough room to buffer you from your neighbors.

I know a married couple who thought they wanted solitude on their weekends. They bought a remote tract of land in northern Minnesota and built a self-sufficient cabin. The cabin was their pride and joy while they were building it, with the help of friends. The first few weekends after completing the cabin, the couple would drive to their camp to get away from it all. Quickly they found out that they really didn't want solitude. They could not stand being without people, stores, and human activity in general. They spent most of their weekends shopping in small towns in the area, looking for events to attend, and driving to a nearby hill where they could call friends on their cell phone. They sold the cabin they were so proud of and bought another one just outside the city limits of the town where they lived. They do enjoy cabin living, but not solitude.

Site selection begins by deciding on what geographical setting—lakes, mountains, seashore—you want for your dream cabin.                    Photo by JWF

I advise anyone who wants to build a cabin for solitude to first rent a cabin
in a remote location and give solitude a real try before spending time, money,
and effort to build a cabin in a really remote location. Not long ago I had a
friend stay with me for several days at my cabin. On the third morning as we
sat on the porch watching a flock of wild turkeys feeding on a distant ridge, my
friend asked, "How do you stand not having visitors for days at a time?" He
missed the whole point. Solitude is great for some, but it's not for everyone.

## IN WHAT REGION DO YOU WANT YOUR CABIN?

Having written down a detailed description of your ideal cabin setting, decided on how much land you really need, and knowing whether you want an
isolated cabin, we are ready next to target a geographical region to begin the
land search. If you want your cabin within commuting distance of your
home, then you are probably living in or close to the geographical region.

If you don't know, then you must correlate your idea of what is "in the woods" with a geographical region. Perhaps climate is important to you. "In the woods" to you might be the cool summer temperatures of the mountains or ice-skating on a remote lake. Knowing what you want in the way of your cabin setting will give you some idea as to the region you should consider. If you know of a particular lake, stream, or mountain range that speaks to you, then you already know the geographical area in which to search. Most tourist information bureaus can give you specific information as to regions of their state if you tell them the type of setting you want. State travel departments also have web sites in addition to glossy brochures.

Once you have selected one or more regions to explore, contact the chambers of commerce of towns and cities found in the region. Usually their web sites will give the climate information and much more data that is of use in beginning a search for land.

## BUYING OR LEASING?

There once was a time when many large landowners such as paper companies, utility companies, insurance companies, and lumber companies would give an individual cabin builder an inexpensive long term lease on a small tract of land. Even some government land management agencies got in on the act. In most of the country, these days are over, especially with government agencies. While there are still some companies that do lease land for cabin building it is no longer cheap, and there may be a clause in the lease that allows the company to terminate the lease on short notice. In addition, many leases are written so that the company dictates what type and size cabin you can build and what activities you can do on the land. The best advice I can give you on leasing land for building a permanent cabin is to have an attorney review any lease and explain it to you in detail. Know what you are getting into: How long is the lease for, what is the termination policy, and who owns the cabin at termination? Compare their rules with your goals and desires, and know all costs associated with the lease.

Also, find out for sure what the company plans on doing with the land adjacent to your lease tract. I know of cases where soon after a family leased a tract on which to build their dream cabin, the company clear-cut the timber on the adjacent land. On another lease, two couples that leased a lakefront tract learned after starting their cabin that the lake was to be drained for three years for dam renovation. Find out long-term plans and uses of the property around the potential land for lease, and incorporate some protection into your lease.

While I am sure there are still some good leasing opportunities out there, I prefer to own the land my cabin sits on so that I control the development of, and the future of my cabin. It may be a bit of a strain to pay for the land and cabin in the beginning, but I have never had a cabin that wasn't a good investment. As I said earlier, a cabin and the land it sits on is an ongoing project never quite finished, and it would be a shame to have to give up that investment of time and money in twenty or so years. A cabin should be something you leave to the kids or grandchildren. It is a family heritage and will be rare before this new century is over.

While we are on the subject of finding land, I still see ads for free or "very cheap" Alaskan or Canadian lands. Usually to get this information there is a fee involved. The days of free homestead lands are over. I spend a lot of time in Alaska and Canada, and I have not seen any free or cheap land suitable for cabin building in years. In addition, the ads for "cheap" land in the Western states should be looked upon with equal caution. Not many people want a cabin in a desert where there is no water. Most of the people running these ads make their money off the fees collected by those who purchase the information.

## SHOULD YOU HAVE A PARTNER?

Buying land and building a cabin doesn't have to be expensive, but it does cost more and requires more work than many things we normally do. To help cut the cost and share the workload, a few people I know have taken on partners or sold interests in the project. While this works on occasion, more often than not, it ends up being an unpleasant experience that leads to the property being sold or disputes being settled in court, and in both cases, friends often become enemies. My advice is that if there is any way you can swing the deal alone, do it alone. Let the friends enjoy helping you with the work, and invite them to spend a weekend at the cabin occasionally.

Irving Price, in his best-selling book *Buying Country Property,* said it best: "The initial concept to purchase jointly a country place may appear simple and advantageous, but the hazards are many. An attorney should be consulted before joining hands and dancing around the mulberry bush. You may be assured that your council will advise formal agreement setting forth in detail the respective rights and obligations of all concerned with each phase of the purchase, its use, improvements, resale of all or part, individual personal liability, estate involvement, financing, and decision-making policies."

He continued, "Our files contain the histories of hundreds of joint-purchase prospective clients who initially started their search for country property with every good and honorable intention. But along the grueling way of noncompromise and disagreement, the decision was reached to go it alone and live happily ever after."

## Finding Land—Be Patient

You have a good idea as to the type and amount of land you need for your cabin, the general location or region, and a budget as to what you can afford to spend. Now you are ready to begin the search. The first caution here is to be patient, and don't settle for anything less than what you really want. Many dream cabins have turned into bad dreams because the builders rushed into buying land that did not turn out to be what they really wanted.

An example of where rushing shattered a dream was a businessman from the South Carolina coast who wanted a mountain cabin to escape the heat and humidity of the coastal summers. He chose the mountains of northwestern South Carolina, because they were within easy driving distance of his home. All his life he had dreamed of having a rustic cabin on a hilltop where he could sit outside and watch the sun go down. He did not do much research about the summer climate in the hill country in which he bought a small hilltop tract of land, surrounded by large pine trees. He spent winter weekends with his sons building the cabin he had always wanted. The cabin was completed in late spring, and the owner planned a summer vacation there for the following July.

July came, and the new owner and his family arrived at the cabin to find that all the beautiful trees on the neighboring land had been clear-cut. His cabin sat on a hot, dry hill with only the trees on his three acres to give any relief from the hot July South Carolina sun. The humidity was just as bad as where he lived, and it was too hot to sit outside and watch the sunset. They did not stay there the entire week. I helped him sell the cabin later that year.

Had this gentleman been patient and studied the region a little more, he could have found a tract of land a little farther up the road where the mountains reach a cool three to four thousand feet in elevation. In addition, he could have found a site where the adjacent land was not going to be clear-cut. Take the time to enjoy the search for that "just right" piece of property, and don't settle for anything less.

## SEARCHING ON YOUR OWN

If you have friends or family in the chosen region, or you have experience in buying rural land, then you may want to begin searching for land on your own rather than working with a realtor. I have found that spending a few days in the county seat of the county you are interested in can be very valuable. Pick up copies of the local newspapers and look for tracts of land that are for sale. Get brochures and sale booklets from local real estate companies. This can help familiarize you with the price of land in the region.

Two of the most valuable sources of information in any area are the county agricultural extension office (county agent) and the Natural Resource and Conservation Service (NRCS) office. Both of these agencies work with rural landowners. They know the land and might know of someone willing to sell you the place of your dreams. These agencies usually have offices in the county courthouse or county agricultural office center. Their services are free.

You can take out an ad in the local newspaper describing the type of land you are looking for, and you will hear from willing sellers. I have done this but was disappointed with the results. Most of those who responded to the ad either overpriced their land or tried to sell me land that wasn't really what I wanted.

If you are looking for a lease lot, then you will want to get in touch with the company or government agency that has made it known that they have land available for lease. Usually you will be dealing with a forester or land manager, and the price is usually fixed with little or no room for negotiating. Farmers and ranchers have been known to lease land for long periods to those wanting to build a cabin, but most will want to sell land rather than lease. Talk to the county agent and NRCS agent about leasing from rural landowners in your region of interest.

The more people you get to know in the area and talk to about what type of property you have in mind, the better the odds are you will hear from someone who has exactly what you are looking for. Be sure to take along plenty of business cards or cards stating your phone, fax, and e-mail address to leave with those you meet on your visits to the area.

## WORKING WITH A REAL ESTATE AGENT

If all of this is new to you and/or you do not have contacts in the region you have chosen, then you should consider getting a good real estate agent to help you with your search. You will want an agent experienced in rural land. A realtor's knowledge of the rural property in the area can save you a lot of time. To find a good one, ask around as to what real estate agent handles the most raw land sales. Ask a banker, county agent, and farm supply dealer for recommendations.

Remember that the real estate agent works for the seller. Make sure the agent that you choose knows what you are looking for and the price range you can afford. A good agent will search diligently to find the land you want and in the process save you time.

## LOOKING AT PROPERTY

At last, you have found a tract of land that sounds like what you have been looking for. Before you visit the property, find out exactly where it is located. For this a USGS topographical map and an aerial photograph would be most helpful. You can download a copy of the topo map that includes the property from www.maptech.com, or you can purchase a topo map from the United States Geological Survey at www.usgs.gov. Topo maps are usually available at local sporting goods stores and map dealers. You can download an aerial photograph from www.terraserver.com, or you may obtain a copy from a local Natural Resource and Conservation Service office.

The USGS topo map gives you an aerial view of the earth's surface and uses contour lines to portray the shape and elevation of the land. Topo maps show both natural and manmade features. They show and name works of nature including mountains, valleys, lakes, rivers, swamps, open areas, and vegetation. They also identify the principal works of man, such as roads, political boundaries, transmission lines, and buildings. As you can see, an up-to-date 7.5-minute topo, at a scale of 1 inch equals 2,000 feet, will give you a good idea as to how the property you are going to visit and the surrounding area actually look on the ground. Bring the topo with you when looking at cabin property, so that you can pencil notes on the map or margins.

On this first visit, leave your checkbook at home, but bring a notebook and pen with you. As the real estate agent or landowner shows you the property, or soon after, make a list of the things you like and don't like about it.

Observe the access to the property, and find out what the access road conditions are like during heavy snow or rain. Ask the person showing you the property to point out potential building sites. Ask whether there are any easements or rights of way through the property.

## TO BUY OR NOT TO BUY?

The first visit will likely be short. If you have had a day or two to think about the property and study your notes, and you still think this is your dream location, set up a second visit and make it a daylong or even a weekend visit if possible. Start by driving around the property's environs and noting what's going on in the surrounding countryside. Is there a hog farm upwind from the property? Are developments encroaching the countryside in the area? Is it in the path of urban sprawl? If there are forested areas adjacent to the property, are there any signs of recent or imminent logging activity? If there is a stream running through the property, what is on the stream above the tract? Is the property in an area known for avalanches, floods, runoffs, or other natural events that would have an impact?

This is your investment, so don't be bashful about asking about the property and surrounding area. Ask the local forest ranger, conservation officers, county agent, NRCS agent, county health department, sheriff's department, etc. Try to find problems. If you can't, then you are probably on the right track and the property is worth a closer look.

If this is a family project, take the family with you. They may see things that you don't that could make the difference in the future happiness of cabin ownership.

Once again, take along your notepad, topo map, aerial photograph, and by now you should have obtained a copy of the property survey. Walk the boundaries of the property. As you walk around the property, look for potential cabin sites. Observe whether there are any swamps, poorly drained areas, or potential flooding of streams. Note any open meadows, forested areas, and what condition the trees are in, paying attention to views, rocks and soils, and suitable slopes (we will take a closer look at this in the next section).

Now is the time to become aware of everything that is good or bad about the property. Remember, there is a lot of free help available if you just ask for it. Water and sewage questions go to the county health department; drainage, soil, erosion, and stream questions should be directed to the

NRCS agent; forestry questions to the state or district forest ranger; general land management and climate questions to the county extension office; wildlife management questions to the state conservation officer, local/district game warden, or wildlife biologist.

When talking to these people, ask the tough questions about the area: Are there problems with trespassing or vandalism? What is the crime rate? Who maintains the roads, how often do they flood, and how well are they kept open in the winter and after storms? Unfortunately, some forested areas of this country are vulnerable to illegal activities such as dumping garbage, cutting of firewood, trespass hunting, timber theft, breaking into cabins, and general vandalism. Where this occurs it has usually been going on for generations, and you don't want to build your dream cabin there.

An Atlanta doctor I know bought a beautiful tract of wooded land with a small lake on it, but she didn't check out the neighborhood very carefully. She cleaned up the lake and restocked it with fish, and her husband had a nice cabin built near the shore. The first weekend they arrived at the property to enjoy it, their cabin had been vandalized and the lake had been drained (the gate on the dam had been removed). Local lowlifes had stolen everything they

Select the exact site you would like to build the cabin. When seriously considering a tract of land, visit the cabin site several times. Go to the trouble to stake out a cabin footprint to make sure you know what you are getting.

Photo by Mark Thomas

could get. The area was well known for that type of activity, and if the doctor had done her homework, she would have known better than to buy there.

Think of the future and see if your peace and quiet will be threatened. Our present cabin is surrounded on three sides by the national forest.

## THE CABIN SITE

While walking the property, try to pick out the best cabin site and stake an approximate footprint of the size cabin you intend to build. How much land preparation will be necessary? Is the ground satisfactory for footings? Do you have the views you want? If there is no existing access road or driveway into the site, how much will it cost to put one in? Is there adequate drainage around the site? How secure is your site? (I believe in the old saying "Out of sight out of mind.") A good cabin site, to me, is one that isn't visible to passersby, to avoid inviting trouble. These are the kind of questions you should ask as you stake out the cabin site. Move the stakes around until you find a position you really like. Use good common sense.

If there is already an old home site or cabin site on the property, give it consideration, as the people who chose that particular site many years ago

When considering cabin sites, never overlook old cabin or home sites, as these people had a reason for building where they did.                    Photo by JWF

Camping on a prospective site is a good way to determine whether you really want to build your cabin there.                    Photo by the Coleman Company.

likely had a reason for the selection. It may have been because the site was a spring or other water source, or protected from the winter wind; it may have been because it had good drainage during the wet season, or a constant summer breeze to blow away the mosquitoes. Try to visualize why this site was selected. It could save you a lot of time searching for the perfect site.

I like to go back to a proposed cabin site and camp there for a few days, during more than one season if possible, to see if it really is what I want. This has helped me avoid bad decisions several times.

Assuming you like the property and the building site, you have more research to do. A good water supply is critical to a good cabin site (see chapter 15). Where will you get your water? From a drilled well, public water run to the site, a spring somewhere on the property, or will you bring treated drinking and cooking water with you and use stream or lake water for washing dishes and other non-consumptive uses?

In addition, whether you plan on having a modern bathroom or an outhouse (chapter 10), there will be regulations you will have to follow.

The answers to both of these issues are available at the county health department. Be sure to check these out early. It's too late after you have bought the property to learn that the well water in the area contains lots of sulfur, or a well deep enough to get a good supply of water will cost several times what you thought, or the site for your cabin will not pass a percolation test for the bathroom you planned for the cabin.

Next, you will want to check out the availability of any utilities you may want to run to your cabin. Electricity, gas, and water may or may not be available, and the cost can vary. Check these out before you buy.

If you choose a small self-sufficient cabin, much of this work will not be necessary.

## CLOSING THE DEAL

You have visited the property many times. You have picked out the cabin site and you know it is what you want. You have looked into utilities, water supply, sanitary regulations, roads, and everything checks out. Now is the time to get your attorney involved.

Have your attorney review the deed: Are you buying all rights or just surface rights? Is the title clear and can you get title insurance? Are there any contracts, such as timber cutting or hunting rights that you must abide by? Is the survey current and was it done by a certified surveyor? Paying a *good* attorney to make sure all these and other details are taken care of is money well spent. Also you will want your attorney to examine or write the purchase and sales agreement, especially if there are clauses stating that the closing is subject to certain criteria, such as finding good well water or getting an easement across a neighbor's land. Now you are ready to purchase your cabin site.

3

# The Look You Want

Planning a cabin takes some time, but it is fun. The next few chapters will be about planning what style and size cabin you want. However, before we begin, let's first decide what type of materials we are going to use on the outside and inside of the cabin. The exterior and interior materials give the cabin the look you want and its strength.

One of the great things about simple backcountry-style cabin plans is that they can be built using a wide variety of building materials. I have seen cabins made from soft drink bottles, bricks, logs, tin, adobe, rocks, planks, plywood, sawmill outside cuts, wooden pallets, flattened aviation fuel cans—and the list could go on for pages. Resourceful people in remote places can take just about anything and make a small cabin from it, especially if cold weather is on the way.

In this book, we are only going to consider the most popular of cabin building materials, wood. Whether it is in the form of logs, plywood, boards, or log siding, wood is readily available, looks at home in the backcountry, and is easy to work with. Even the beginning cabin builder can soon become relatively adept at building with wood. I am living proof. If I can build a cabin, anyone can, as my building skills are somewhat limited. I have built cabins out of all these wood materials, and the cabins looked good, gave comfortable shelter, and years later are still standing and serviceable.

For the shell of your cabin, we will look at four types of exterior siding materials that are among the best and the most rustic in appearance.

## LOGS—THE ULTIMATE BUILDING
## MATERIAL FOR BACKCOUNTRY CABINS

Probably all who dream of a cabin in the woods started out with the image of a log cabin. Solid logs are a great building material, as they do a good job of insulating a cabin when properly erected. The inside wall goes up when the exterior wall goes up. Logs are also more fireproof than many people think. If you can cut them on your own property, they are inexpensive; and when there is some skilled help available, they go up quickly. A log cabin simply looks good, like it belongs in the backcountry setting.

Logs that are not cut on the property can be rather expensive. You have to pay someone to cut and trim the logs, possibly season them, and then ship them to your site. If you must then cut the logs to length and notch them, the cost can go up, especially if you need to hire someone with the skill to match and notch logs. If you buy a log home kit, the price will probably go higher, depending upon the package you purchase. Log cabin kits offer a wide range of log types (squared logs, round logs, D-logs), and the way the logs fit together will vary with company and log type. It will be more than just simply ordering logs.

Logs are the ideal choice for cabin building, provided they can be cut on site or the builder is willing to go to the expense to purchase off-site logs.

Photo by JWF

Log siding, as on this New Mexico cabin, looks just like logs and lasts as long, but costs less. Photo by JWF

Logs are an ideal choice of cabin building material if they can be cut on the site, or if you can afford the additional expense of having them cut elsewhere and shipped.

There are many good books and videos available to teach the cabin builder how to build with logs. In addition, many dealers of the packaged log homes offer short courses on building with logs. If you want to learn log-building skills, the educational resources are out there.

## Log Siding

When whole logs are out of the question, then consider using log siding outside and inside as a good second choice. My Cross Creek Hollow cabin has both an exterior and interior of log siding. The rounded 2-by-8-inch Southern yellow pine boards are shaped to look like real logs, and they do, even up close. In fact, two foresters visiting my cabin wanted to know if I cut the logs on the property. Professionals find it hard to tell the difference. Most log siding is of shiplap design so that one board overlaps the next board resulting in a tight fit.

This close-up shows how log siding fits together to give the cabin a tight seal.

Photo by JWF

Building with log siding does not require any special skills or tools. Anyone with carpentry skills can build a cabin using this material. You frame in the cabin and nail the log siding to the frame using twist nails.

Log siding is not cheap, but it costs less than logs and goes up in a hurry. It is available treated or untreated.

## BOARD-AND-BATTEN, AN OLD FAVORITE

The board-and-batten method of nailing rough-cut boards vertically has long been used as a cabin exterior. A wooden strip, or batten, is nailed over each seam. I have read that this style of siding originated in the Scandinavian countries.

There are many advantages to a board-and-batten exterior. Putting the siding up vertically adds to the structural strength of the cabin. With the boards pushed tightly together and a strip of wood nailed over each joint, the cabin is tight, keeping rain and wind out. The siding is easy and quick to

Board-and-batten siding gives a rustic look to your cabin and can be fast and inexpensive to put up.

Photo by JWF

put up. If a sawmill is nearby, you can usually get rough-sawn boards at a very good price. Board-and-batten cabins have a rustic appearance and look like they belong in the backcountry. Some of the best-looking cabins I have seen were constructed with board-and-batten siding.

## REVERSE BOARD-AND-BATTEN

A very good-looking exterior material, and one that goes up quickly, is plywood-type siding that is commonly called reverse board-and-batten. When installed on a cabin it appears to be board-and-batten, but it actually comes as a 4-by-8-foot sheet shaped with a pattern of raised "boards" and recessed "batten" strips.

I built a two-bedroom cabin back in the early 1980s using reverse board-and-batten siding, and the cabin today still looks good and needs no repair. The sheets come in different thicknesses, and I recommend a thickness of ½ inch or more for cabin exteriors. The siding is not inexpensive, but it can save you the difference in labor, as it is one of the easiest to put up. It is also tough, weather resistant, and looks just as good as a real board-and-

Reverse board-and batten, as used on this Oregon cabin, comes in 4-by-8-foot sheets and can speed up cabin construction.                    Photo by JWF

batten cabin. In addition, it makes a great interior wall covering inside cabins and can take a lot of wear and tear. There are many other materials to use on the exterior of a cabin, however these are among the best and the most rustic in appearance.

## PROTECTING THE EXTERIOR

Your cabin is a valuable investment, both in terms of money and time, so you will want it to last, trouble-free, as long as possible. As soon as the wooden shell of your cabin is complete, deterioration will begin in the form of mold, mildew, UV rays, fungus, wood rot, termites, and boring insects. The best way to discourage these pests is to protect your cabin siding from the beginning by treating it with a wood preservative. It is not difficult to do and it is a small price to pay for many years of problem-free living.

Thanks to modern chemistry, there are many excellent products available on the market that make this an easy task. Companies such as Perma-Chink, Sashco, and Weatherall, to name a few, offer a wide variety of

Protecting the exterior of your cabin will help keep your cabin looking new and prevent mold, mildew, and fungus from taking hold.                    Photo by JWF

products for the cabin builder. Many are environmentally safe, and this is important in the backcountry setting.

When we were building our Cross Creek Hollow cabin, we used Perma-Chink products, and have used them since for periodic maintenance. After ten years of hard use, the cabin is as good as new. Other companies have similar products, and they can recommend the best procedure for using their products.

When the exterior was going up, I sprayed Perma-Chink's Shell-Guard on the log siding. This product was developed for logs, but I have found that it works well on any exterior wood product. It penetrates the wood, using moisture present to travel through the wood to reach fungi and wood-destroying insects. I sprayed it on using a 3-gallon plastic garden sprayer.

To enhance the color of the siding and to protect it from damaging UV rays, I brushed on a coat of autumn gold Lifeline Ultra-1 stain. This finish is semitransparent and allows the grain of the wood to show through. Then I sealed the stain with a coat of clear Lifeline Proguard. The results have been very good.

I recently restored a very discolored log outbuilding using the same procedure, with one exception. First, to get the logs back to their natural color, I sprayed on a coat of Olympic Deck Cleaner and allowed it to sit a few minutes, then washed it off with water. I was amazed at how well this product worked. After the logs dried I treated them, following the same procedure as described above, and the log building looked new again.

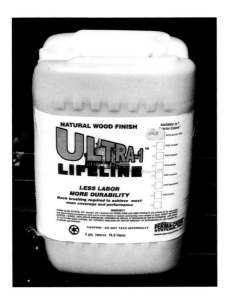

The author used Perma-Chink Ultra-1 Lifeline for protecting the siding of his Cross Creek Hollow cabin.

Photo by JWF

While the process of applying these finishes is fairly straightforward, I will offer the following tips:

1. Read carefully and follow to the word the instructions that come with the products you choose to use. Don't hesitate to call the manufacturer's customer service department if you need help. These products are not cheap and work well when properly used.
2. Clean all work surfaces carefully.
3. Apply products at moderate temperatures, 45 to 90 degrees Fahrenheit.
4. Be sure to allow previous applications time to thoroughly dry before applying the next coat.
5. Good tools lead to good work. Avoid using old leaky sprayers, worn-out paintbrushes, and the like. Make sure it is safe to use the sprayer you have for the product you are spraying. Be sure to follow all of the manufacturer's safety instructions.
6. Don't rush. Your cabin's look and protection are at stake. Take your time. Make the job fun.

## ROOFING

The type of roofing material you decide to put on your cabin will have as much to do with the cabin's finished look as the exterior siding. The most common choices are cedar shakes, metal roofing, or composite shingles. In most cases cedar shakes, even though they really look good on many cabin designs, are ruled out due to the fire hazard from forest fires and sparks from wood-burning stoves or fireplaces.

Composite shingles are a good choice of roofing provided the roofers who put them up are skilled, the shingles selected are of a high grade, and they match the exterior of the cabin. Today there is a good selection of composite shingles that look like cedar or slate shakes. The brand name of a product I have used on several cabins is CertainTeed Shangle. (www.certain-teed.com.) The Shangle is a heavyweight shingle that consists of a minimum of two full-sized shingles laminated together, giving it a shake-like appearance. They are strong and will last for decades under normal use.

Metal roofing is a good choice of roofing material for remote cabins. When properly installed it offers the qualities of being strong but lightweight, fire resistant, wind resistant, hail resistant, engineered to be permanent, adds value to older cabins, and can be expected to last the life of the building. It can be purchased in a variety of colors, and is relatively easy and quick to install.

The most common metal roofing used on cabins is standing-seam panels. They make a great roof and are virtually maintenance free. I have such a roof on my cabin, and in ten years, I have only had to tighten two screws. The roof still looks new. For more information on panel metal roofs, go to the web site, www.metalroofingspecialist.com.

At one time, most cabins with metal roofs had panel roofs, but now there is a quality steel shingle roofing that is going on a lot of cabins. They have the good looks of cedar shakes with the quality of a metal roof. For more information go to the web site, www.metalworksroof.com.

Your cabin's exterior look will be important to you, and will make a first impression on those who visit your cabin. Take your time when deciding on exterior wall materials, finishes, and roofing, as you will have to live with them a long time. They help give your cabin its personality.

A metal roof looks natural on a cabin and if properly installed will give years of trouble-free service.                                            Photo by JWF

CHAPTER

4

# The Simple Adirondack
# Shelter

I have a good friend who has a nice one-room cabin located at the end of a twisting dirt road in the mountains of Virginia. I was visiting him one weekend, and as I walked around admiring his new cabin, we talked about trout fishing on a remote creek that was higher in the mountains. "How would you like to hike up to the creek tomorrow for a little fishing and stay in my secret cabin?" he asked. I couldn't say yes fast enough, not so much for the fishing, but to see a cabin I had never heard about.

The next afternoon, after a long hike, we reached the headwaters of the creek. It was in a gorge and looked as if no one had ever been there before. I wondered as we walked upstream how he ever got the materials in here to build a cabin. We rounded a bend in the creek, and on a knoll above the creek, I saw his secret cabin. It was an Adirondack lean-to made of logs. In front of the shelter was a well-made reflector fire pit made of rocks. It was one of the most inviting camps I think I have ever seen. We spent the cool night there as comfortably as if we were in a house. We were warm, had plenty of fresh air, and could enjoy the blaze of the fire. I wanted to stay a few more days.

The Adirondack shelter, sometimes referred to as a three-sided cabin, Appalachian Trail lean-to, or Adirondack lean-to, was born out of necessity when the American frontier was Vermont and New York. These shelters were probably first built by Native Americans of the area, but it didn't take long for the early explorers and settlers of the region to realize their value. Records show that many settlers used this type of shelter as their first home, and expanded it into a larger cabin as time permitted. I have read that a family would build a large Adirondack for the first winter on a homestead, and during the next summer build a second one facing the first, with the fire in

31

Adirondack shelters have served as remote cabins for several centuries and still serve today as an easy-to-build, trouble-free shelter.                Photo by JWF

In early America, and occasionally today, Adirondacks are converted into more permanent structures.                Photo by JWF

the middle. The third year they would roof the opening between the two and wall-in the sides. It became a much larger cabin.

Adirondacks have been in use ever since those early days and with good reason. When properly built and situated on a site, they make a comfortable shelter. They are inexpensive to build and last for years. Back in the mid 1930s, eleven log Adirondack shelters were built along the Appalachian Trail in Maine. Today six of those shelters are still in use. All along the Appalachian Trail, from Maine to Georgia, there are dozens of these shelters that get hard use year after year and are still very comfortable.

Today the Adirondack shelter has found its way throughout North America. I visited with a Cree Indian couple in the Cassier Mountains of British Columbia and stayed in the Adirondack shelter that served as their summer home. One of the most comfortable elk camps I have ever enjoyed had Adirondack shelters for its base camp, and two of the guides lived year-round in the shelters.

## THE ADIRONDACK AS A CABIN

I felt that the Adirondack shelter belonged in a book about backcountry cabins. It is an ideal shelter for remote locations where use and/or materials may not justify a full-blown cabin. The Adirondack would be an economical starter cabin for someone on a tight budget. I am building one on a creek near our Cross Creek Hollow cabin for use during hot summer nights and as a base camp to teach my grandchildren outdoor skills. The Adirondack gives you the comfort of a cabin but requires the use of camping skills and knowledge, offering more of an outdoor experience. In short, the Adirondack is an outstanding shelter that is a lot of fun to build and to live in.

With a shelter that is open on one side, orientation is especially important. To have an Adirondack shelter that is comfortable year-round, you'll need to locate the open side of the shelter opposite to the direction of the prevailing winds and storms. In other words, you want the shelter built with its back to the wind.

A second trick is to build a fire pit off the open side of the shelter so that a reflector fire can be built during cold weather. When a reflector fire is built in front of the Adirondack, it becomes an oven of sorts. The sloping roof catches the heat and throws it downward into the shelter. I have stayed in Adirondacks in sub-freezing weather and been very comfortable as long as the fire was tended. If you don't know how to build a reflector fire, check out a camping book and learn before you build your Adirondack. It's simple to master.

## BUILDING AN ADIRONDACK SHELTER

Many Adirondack shelters are built in remote locations inaccessible to trucks, so by necessity are usually built from logs cut on the site. When clearing trees for an Adirondack site, it is best to try to take as many logs as you can. People are usually surprised at how many logs it takes to build an Adirondack shelter. To build an average-sized Adirondack shelter 12 feet across the front and 8 feet deep, a size that can sleep up to six people comfortably, can take up to 60 logs averaging 8 inches in diameter. Even with the logs cut on site, you will still need to pack in tools, hardware, and other building materials, such as roofing.

The logs should be cut between July and August so that they peel easily. Trimming and peeling should be done when the trees are cut. Then the logs should be allowed to dry for six weeks before the shelter is built.

This modern-day Adirondack shelter can be built quickly and easily and serves all the fundamental needs.                                    Photo by JWF

I could spend the next dozen or so pages telling you how to build an Adirondack shelter out of logs, but that would take away from the planning theme of the book. An excellent 64-page how-to booklet can be purchased from the Maine Appalachian Trail Club (P.O. Box 283, Augusta, ME 04330) or the Appalachian Trail Conference (P.O. Box 807, Harpers Ferry, WV 25425).

My good friend Chris Drew, Chief Ranger at Baxter State Park in Maine, builds an Adirondack shelter out of log siding that is most comfortable and easy to construct. It is simply framed in and then the log siding is nailed on. The roof can be composition roofing or metal roofing. The raised floor of the shelter serves as a sleeping platform that puts the users off the ground and closer to heat during cold-weather use. A family could construct one of these shelters during a long weekend. It will give years of service with a little periodic maintenance.

While the Adirondack is not a true cabin, it is a great temporary cabin, especially in remote areas, and would make a good shelter to build on your cabin site to stay in while you build the main cabin. It makes a great woodshed, overflow guest quarters, tool shed or equipment building when the cabin is complete.

## ADVANTAGES OF THE ADIRONDACK SHELTER:

- It is an ideal shelter for remote locations where full-sized cabins are not feasible.
- It is very quick and easy to build, with little help necessary.
- Often it can be built from logs cut on the site, and can be used for other purposes later.
- It offers the basic comfort of a small cabin, yet allows the use of camping skills.
- It is the most affordable permanent shelter, and requires little maintenance.

# CHAPTER 5

# The Alaskan Trapper's–Style Cabin

I have written many magazine articles about different styles of backcountry cabins, always a popular subject. However, the articles I have written about the Alaskan trapper's–style cabins seem to draw the most interest, usually in the form of hundreds of letters from readers wanting to build one of the cabins.

This style of cabin has a lot going for it, especially if you want to build a cabin that is going to be self-sufficient, with no electricity, phone lines, or indoor plumbing. Aside from the cabin's pleasing aesthetics, it is simple in design, highly efficient for backwoods living, inexpensive to build, and can be built quickly.

This trapper's-style cabin usually has a steep roof with the ridgepole running from front to back. The roof continues in front of the cabin to provide shelter for a good-sized porch. The cabin should be rectangular from front to rear, not square. It is the cabin design most often associated with Alaskan bush living, and with good reason; it is a darned good design.

## BUILDING A ONE-ROOM TRAPPER'S-STYLE CABIN

Here is the story of how I built my current Alaskan trapper's–style cabin. Many of the construction features I used here will apply to the other cabins discussed in this book.

In 1990, I decided it was time to construct my own Alaskan trapper's–style cabin on some remote land I owned adjacent to a national forest in the mid-South. My cabin budget would be limited to $8,000, including outhouse and woodshed, and I had a set of design criteria that I felt

The Alaskan trapper's–style cabin is one of the best designs for those wanting a totally self-sufficient structure.                                    Photo by JWF

were a must for my cabin. It had to be comfortable for four adults. Due to the wide range of weather extremes in the mountains at my cabin site, it had to be energy-efficient. I would warm it in the winter with a small catalytic-converter wood-burning stove and keep it comfortable in the hot summers by means of a high ceiling and cross-ventilation from screened windows.

I wanted the cabin to have a log cabin appearance but preferred stud wall framing for simplicity of construction. Since there was no electricity near the cabin site, the design had to be such that all power tools used in construction could be operated from my Coleman portable 175-watt generator. The cabin must also be comfortable and efficient without the luxuries of electricity and running water.

To give me more time for outdoor recreation, it was necessary that my cabin be as maintenance-free as possible with minimal opening and closing time. I also wanted the outhouse to be clean, bright, and odor-free. Finally, the design had to be such that I could do most of the construction myself with a minimum of professional help.

I knew this was a tall order for a small cabin, but after many nights spent studying cabins I had used in the past and drawing floor plans over and over, I came up with a simple design for a one-room, 16-by-20-foot

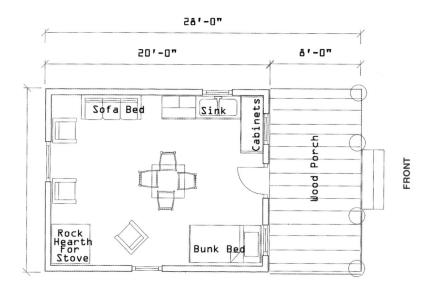

Illustration and floor plan of the one-room Alaskan-style cabin.

Photo by JWF

cabin with an 8-by-16-foot front porch. The exterior and interior walls would be made from 2-by-8-inch log siding, and the roof would be 26-gauge metal roofing with a baked-on, siliconized polyester finish. With plans in hand, I was ready to start.

The site I chose on the property was perfect. I call the acreage Cross Creek Hollow because of the five creeks crisscrossing it. You have to cross a creek to go anywhere. The cabin would be built in a deep hollow with a spring-fed creek running down one side. Tall hills give the cabin protection from cold winter winds. The same heavily wooded hills also offer shade most of the day during the summer. Since the hollow was once a remote horse pasture, the yard around the cabin was already well sodded in grass.

I decided to build my cabin on railroad crosstie piers to allow air to move freely under it. Not only would this help keep it cool in the summer, but would protect it from flooding because, according to my research, the creek adjacent to the cabin was subject to get out of its banks occasionally. If flash floodwaters reached the cabin, I wanted them to meet little resistance. The NRCS agent figured the 100-year flood potential, and I designed the floor to be above that level.

## Starting Construction

The first step was to set 12 crosstie piers 4 feet into the ground in concrete, with the top elevation three feet from the ground to keep the floor joists above any possible floods in the future. I gave the piers a few days to set up.

Working with a forest ranger friend who has carpentry skills, we put in pressure-treated 2-by-8-inch floor joists with 16-inch centers. To keep the cabin as insect-proof as possible and to protect the subfloor from ground moisture, we tightly stapled a sheet of 4mm polyethylene film to the top of the floor joists. Over that, we stapled a layer of felt roll roofing. Next, we laid 10 sheets of 7⁄16-inch wafer board for the subfloor. For floor insulation, a friend had traded me several sheets of four-inch-thick plastic foam insulation, and we cut these into strips and nailed them tightly into place between floor joists on the bottom of the subflooring.

With the subflooring completed, I hired two carpenters to frame-in the cabin, put the roof on, and set in the windows. I knew it was critical that these jobs be done right, and they accomplished the chore in a fraction of the time I would have spent struggling with them. The walls were framed with 2-by-4 studs on 16-inch centers, and the rafters were 2-by-8s on 16-inch centers.

To help keep the cabin cool during the hot Southern summers and to provide a potential sleeping loft, the cabin has a cathedral ceiling with a height of 12 feet at the peak. This also gives the interior a spacious feeling.

Since you must tie beams of some sort across the long walls to prevent the walls from spreading apart, I used two 8-inch rough-peeled logs as beams. They add to the rustic look of the interior and, with a few nails added, make a good place for hanging skillets, lanterns, and wet socks.

To support the front porch's roof, I used four 6-inch red cedar logs that came from my boyhood home place, with the bark left on. As the cabin neared completion, I added porch rails, which came from one of my former hunting lodge properties, made of 3-inch red cedar poles with the bark left on to give it a backwoods touch. The porch floor was made from 1-by-6 pressure-treated boards.

I bought the best heavy-gauge metal I could find for the roof. It has a baked-on green finish to blend in with the woods and won't require maintenance for years. It's also cozy on rainy nights, listening to the patter of rain on the roof.

My cross-ventilation air conditioning was accomplished by placing two windows in the front of the cabin to take advantage of the cooling north breeze in the summer, a window over the kitchen sink on the right side of the cabin, and a fourth window on the creek side of the structure. Since I

The author's cabin was built using standard framing construction covered with log siding inside and out.                                    Photo by JWF

had planned to add a stove and bunks on the back wall, I didn't add windows on that side. The windows were prehung and had screens so they could be opened in the warm months without inviting in the insects.

## Putting Up the Log Siding

With the cabin framed in, I began adding the exterior log siding. This went up quickly and tightly. As I mentioned earlier, I used log siding inside and out, and many visitors think the cabin is a solid-log structure.

Once the exterior walls were up, I stapled roll roofing on the inside of the exterior wall to help make it insect, moisture, and wind proof. Next, I insulated the walls with R-11 fiberglass insulation and the ceiling with R-19 fiberglass insulation. I took extra care to insulate possible sources of heat loss, such as around the door and windows.

The interior walls were then covered with the log siding and the ceiling was decked with 11 sheets of knotty, ½-inch CD plywood. This gave the ceiling a rustic look that went well with the log walls.

My forest ranger friend made the front door out of 2-by-8-inch boards while I completed the floor. On top of the subfloor, I put down a layer of roll roofing. Over that, I nailed down handpicked 1-by-7-inch pine boards. The wood floor was finished with three coats of honey-pine polyurethane stain.

One of the carpenters who framed the cabin is also a rock mason, and in one corner of the back of the cabin he built a rock hearth and faced two walls 46 inches high and 48 inches out from the corner. This is where I placed the wood-burning stove (more of this in chapter 11).

Along part of two walls in the front of the cabin, I built a cabinet complete with a sink that drains to a grease trap buried outside. I salvaged the sink from a house being torn down, so it didn't cost anything. I wired in two hidden electrical outlets, which I can use with the generator if I desire. To date, they have not been used; everyone who stays in the cabin has preferred our Coleman propane lanterns and kerosene lamps.

The exterior of the cabin was stained and sealed. The roof's 2-foot overhang gives the exterior walls added protection from the elements.

Because I enjoy backcountry cooking, I provided for several means of cooking at the cabin. Inside, I use a Coleman three-burner propane camp stove, a Fox Hill Sport's Oven, and, in winter, the top of the wood-burning stove. I have a permanent fire pit outside where I cook in Dutch ovens and reflector ovens. Behind the cabin, I have built a permanent bean hole

### ALASKAN TRAPPER'S–STYLE ONE-ROOM CABIN
### BILL OF MATERIALS

4,704 lineal feet of 2 x 8 log siding

12 railroad cross-ties, for piers

14 sacks of concrete mix, for setting piers

32 treated 2 x 8 x 10s, for floor joists

17 treated 2 x 8 x 16s, for floor sill

4 prehung windows

11 sheets $1\frac{1}{2}$" CD plywood, for ceiling

35 1 x 6 x 8 treated boards, for porch floor

4 8-foot cedar logs, for porch support

2 peeled cedar logs, for cabin interior

1 roll 4mm polyethylene film

2 rolls of roll roofing

Rocks for stove hearth and hearth walls

2 sacks mortar mix, for hearth

1 sack cement, for hearth

200 pounds brick sand, for hearth

50 wall ties, for hearth

14 rolls fiberglass insulation

90 2 x 4 x 8 studs, for framing

10 sheets $\frac{7}{16}$-inch wafer board, for sub-floor

1 2 x 8 x 12 ridge board

1 2 x 8 x 10 ridge board

20 2 x 4 x 16 fir plates

44 2 x 6 x 12 rafters

42 1 x 6 x 16 pine boards, for floor

Lumber for door

Door hardware

1 box siding nails

1 gallon polyurethane-stain floor finish

1 box galvanized nails

13' high-rib panel, 26-gauge metal roof with baked-on finish

Building materials for author's cabin.

for baking. In addition, I do a lot of grilling and use a smoker. (We'll explore setups for various outdoor and indoor cooking methods in chapters 14 and 16.)

The cabin has no running water. I keep Reliance five-gallon water containers filled with city water brought from home and use this for drinking and cooking. Water for washing dishes, bathing, and cleaning comes from the creek.

I added an outhouse and woodshed, both made with log siding walls to match the cabin, moved the furniture in, and the cabin was ready for use.

The cabin was built for $7,904.29. All my criteria were met, and the cabin has been a hit with everyone who has seen it, and a bigger hit with those who have stayed in it. It has been well tested with as many as six staying in it comfortably. The only problem has been leaving this simple cabin in Cross Creek Hollow when it's time to go home. It is difficult to leave.

## ADDING ON

In 1998, it became apparent that the cabin was not large enough for my growing family. Grandkids were reaching the age to enjoy the cabin and backwoods living, and it was decided that we needed another room. I have stayed in many trapper's cabins that had a second room and knew the addition could be made without ruining the rustic look. So in keeping with the standards I set with the original cabin, I designed a bedroom to be built onto the rear of the structure.

To avoid a "shotgun house" look I stepped the additional bedroom down a bit in size. The dimensions of the additional bedroom are 12 feet wide by 14 feet long. I dropped the ceiling to 10 feet, and used only one log as a cross support, located in the center of the overhead. All construction techniques and materials are the same as the original cabin. A door opening to the room was cut in the back wall of the cabin and a rustic door, designed to match the front door of the original cabin, was made from 2-by-8s. Along the back wall in the new bedroom are three windows, hung side by side. Another two windows are placed on the left and right walls, 28 inches from the back wall. This window arrangement gives lots of light, great cross-ventilation for summer use, and provides plenty of wall space for large bunk beds. This room adds 168 square feet of floor space and sleeps four adults comfortably. The stove in the front room provides plenty of heat for the new bedroom.

The author's cabin, after expansion into a two-room cabin.

Photo by JWF

Due to increased cost in building materials, and because I had to hire more help in building the new room, the addition cost about the same as the original cabin. However, it has been enjoyed so much that I consider it money well spent.

## MORE SPACE

There is a very versatile, larger floor plan for a three-room Alaskan trapper's–style cabin that I like. This plan, counting a front and back porch, measures 40 by 26 feet. It has a large great room/kitchen area and is designed to be heated with a wood-burning stove. There is a 10-by-12 foot pri-

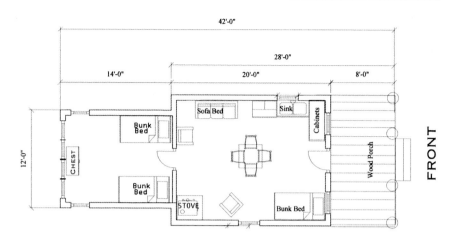

Floor plan for the two-room Alaskan-style cabin.

vate bedroom and a 6-by-8-foot room that could be used as a bathroom, small bunkroom, or storage room. I have stayed in cabins of this design in the backcountry, and usually the small room is used for equipment storage and repair. If the pitch of the roof is steep enough, a sleeping loft can be built over the bedroom/storage room.

This cabin design has a lot of possibilities and could even be a family-size cabin for the family that likes remote locations.

Alaskan Trapper's–Style Cabin
Two-Room

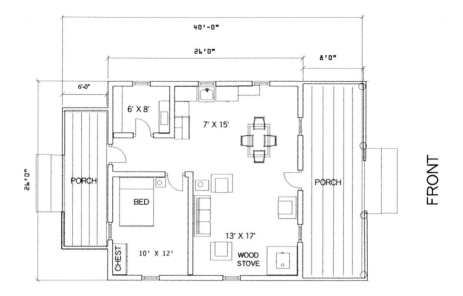

Floor plan for the three-room Alaskan-style cabin.

## A MOVABLE TRAPPER'S-STYLE CABIN

Several years ago I was bear hunting in Alberta, Canada, and spent two weeks in a small trapper's-style cabin that could be moved easily, when the ground was frozen, by hooking it to a farm tractor and sliding it from one location to another. The owner of the cabin built it for use during the winter trapping season and for use by his cowboys when grazing cows in remote areas during the summer. The cabin was small, but it was most comfortable once you got organized. Two of us stayed in the cabin, and enjoyed it even on days of bad weather when we couldn't get out.

The back wall of the cabin is the sleeping area. The bottom bunk is fixed, and the top bunk is hinged to the back wall. When in use the top bunk is pulled down and suspended in place with three chains hooked to the ceiling. When not in use it is pushed back up and locked in place, and the bottom bed serves as a couch. Similarly, a dining/work table is hinged alongside one wall in a location where one occupant can sit on the lower bunk and eat while the other cabin mate sits on a grub box. When not in use the table can be pushed up and locked in place, to make more room in the cabin. A small wood-burning stove is located in the front of the cabin, shar-

The movable trapper's-style cabin.

ing the front wall with the cabin door. To make the cabin brighter and to make it feel larger, slide-open windows are located in the front wall to the right of the door, in the center of the right and left walls, and there are two small windows at the head of each bunk bed. These small windows give reading light on bad-weather days and ventilation in warm weather.

Since then, I have stayed in several similar cabins while doing wildlife management work and hunting in the Arctic. If a small, movable cabin is called for, here is an easy cabin to build. If I were to build one, I would put the bunks along the left wall looking towards the door, with the head of the bed against the front wall, and put the small stove in the back right-hand corner. For safety reasons: I would always like to be between the stove and front door in case of a fire, especially at night.

The foundation is three 8-by-8-inch, 16-foot pressure-treated squared posts. One end of each post is cut on an angle to be placed at the front, with a large eyebolt installed, to slide easily when the cabin is moved. On this foundation, the cabin is built using standard framing techniques. The dimensions of the cabin are 8 by 12 feet. The sidewalls are 8 feet high with the ridge board height of 9 feet. The exterior siding is made from ⅜-inch exterior-grade plywood. The floor, walls, and ceiling are insulated. The interior walls are ⅜-inch plywood painted white to brighten up the inside of the cabin. Roofing material can be metal, composition roofing, or roll roofing. All of these cabins I have stayed in had roll roofing, and it seemed to work fine. The gable ends of the cabin are louvered for ventilation with flaps that can be opened or closed as needed. The front of the cabin has a 4-by-8-foot deck made from pressure-treated 1-by-4-inch boards. During good weather, this deck is used for cooking on a camp stove, washing dishes, or just sitting outside. The sliding windows are made from Plexiglas to prevent them from breaking when the cabin is moved.

When the cabin needs to be moved, pick a day when the ground is frozen. Using the eyebolts in the foundation timbers, hook the cabin to a tractor or bulldozer with a steel cable and slide it to its new setting. One such cabin that I stayed in was located on a marsh, and the owners moved it along the wet grass year-round.

## Advantages of the simple Alaskan trapper's–style cabin with no modern improvements:

- It can be located in remote locations far from utilities and roads.
- It is inexpensive to build, especially if you use logs cut on the site.
- Due to its simple design, it is easy to build, even if your construction skills are limited.
- The self-sufficient design of the cabin makes it a great retreat in emergencies.
- It blends in with the natural surroundings and looks like it belongs there.
- The cabin's high deck serves as a good storage area and is an extension of the cabin's living space during good weather.
- This design is highly efficient for heating during cold weather and sheds snow better than cabins that have roofs with less pitch.
- Like all cabins with few or no modern conveniences, this style of cabin gives the user more of an outdoor experience.

# The Appalachian-Style Cabin

O ne of the oldest and most versatile cabin styles in the United States is the Appalachian-style cabin. To see an excellent collection of these cabins, all you have to do is go to the Great Smoky Mountains National Park and visit Cades Cove or the park's visitor center near Cherokee, North Carolina. Early American settlers used these small but highly efficient cabins to raise large families. The cabin afforded shelter from weather as well as protection from raiding parties.

The Appalachian-style cabin differs from the Alaskan trapper's–style cabin in that the front door is usually in the center of the long side of the cabin and the ridgepole of the roof runs parallel to the front of the cabin. In addition, the porch is on the long side of the cabin and usually runs full length. The porch roof may be separate or it may be a continuation of the cabin roof. Where the Alaskan trapper's–style cabin has a porch with a high ceiling and is usually open in the front, the Appalachian-style cabin porch has a low roof sloping to the front, giving more protection from blowing rain and snow. It may be screened easily, and is a good place to cook and sit during warm weather. I have stayed in cabins of this type where the porch was used for sleeping during hot weather.

Most cabins of this type have a back door and a back porch similar to the front porch. This porch may be screened in to add more covered usable space to the cabin. If the cabin is a self-sufficient cabin, a small table with a washbasin and bucket of water may be available for washing. Often there is a picnic table for fresh-air dining during warm weather. Having two porches adds much to the outside living capacity of the cabin, giving more room inside the structure during much of the year.

The Appalachian-style cabin has served America for centuries and continues to influence the design of cabins today.                    Photo by JWF

Several years ago, I built an Appalachian-style cabin that was 864 square feet in size and was one of the most comfortable cabins I have lived in.

## BUILDING A TWO-ROOM APPALACHIAN-STYLE CABIN

Since the cabin I built was near a road and getting trucks in to the site was easy, I elected to pour a concrete foundation. Once the foundation had hardened, I hired two carpenters to frame the cabin and put on the roof. The roofing material was composition shingles. For the exterior and interior walls, I decided to use reverse board-and-batten. The walls were framed using the same construction guidelines as in my Alaskan trapper's–style cabin in chapter 5. Rather than have cathedral ceilings, however, in this cabin I put in 8-foot ceilings, using sheetrock as a ceiling material, painted white to brighten up the interior. The ceiling was insulated with R-19 fiberglass insulation.

Appalachian Style Cabin
Two-Room

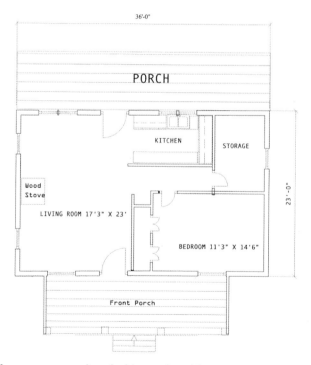

Floor plan for a two-room Appalachian-style cabin.

The two-room cabin was actually divided into four areas—a large living/dining room, a kitchen, a bedroom, and a storage room. If modern conveniences were desired, the storage room could be made into a bathroom without much trouble. All interior walls were made of reverse board-and-batten.

For heating, a rock hearth was built into the living room for a wood-burning Franklin stove. If a fireplace were desired, it could be worked into this plan easily. The lighting, refrigeration, and cooking were designed to use propane from a central system supplied from a large tank located to the rear of the cabin.

To let in light and the beauty from the outdoors, two windows were located along each exterior wall. The best views were to the rear of the cabin; so double windows were hung at the dining area and over the kitchen sink, both along the back wall.

The attic had louvered openings for ventilation, and an entrance was built into the ceiling of the storage room so that it could be accessed for additional storage.

Porch supports were pressure-treated 4-by-4-inch squared beams. The porch railings were made from pressure-treated 2-by-4-inch boards.

## THE TRADITIONAL APPALACHIAN-STYLE CABIN

A traditional Appalachian-style cabin is easy to build and really looks good if built from squared logs. The traditional cabin is a two-story structure with a

Traditional Appalachian Style

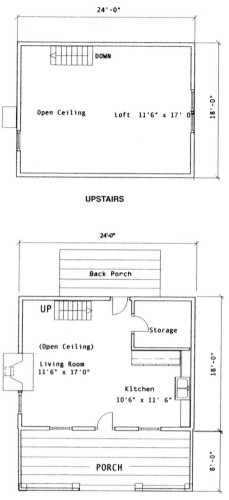

Floor plan for a traditional Appalachian-style cabin with upstairs sleeping loft.

ground floor of 432 square feet and a sleeping loft of 216 square feet. The living room has a vaulted ceiling with exposed rafters, and stairs along the back wall leading to the sleeping loft. A railing runs across the sleeping loft to prevent falls into the living room.

The kitchen and dining area occupies the area under the sleeping loft. The floor plan allows for storage room in the back of the kitchen/dining area or, if modern conveniences are wanted, a bath can be located here.

This cabin is very similar to the cabins used by pioneers in the 1700s and 1800s. It is quick and easy to build and can sleep up to eight people in comfort.

## A ONE-ROOM APPALACHIAN-STYLE CABIN

One of the best examples illustrating just how simple and inexpensive this style cabin is to build is the Appalachian cabin built by a young friend of mine, David Brock.

David had finished high school and attended college, but the "call of the wild" kept him from studying as much as he should. He wanted to go into the woods and build a self-sufficient cabin, from native materials, and basically live off the land. Finally, the urge overcame him, and he made up his mind to give the back-to-the-land lifestyle a try.

Site selection was easy for David. His family had a farm in central Alabama that he had always wanted to live on. There was a wooded hill on the farm, with a spring on it, where David had dreamed of building a cabin. His family gave their approval, and David set about realizing his dream.

His cabin design was a log one-room Appalachian-style that measured 24 by 30 feet. He began by staking out the cabin footprint on the hill. He studied the view from the front porch, the route to the spring, the trees he would cut to build the cabin, and the position of the sun at all hours. David also wanted a good view from the double window he planned to put in the cabin just over his dining/work table. This was important, as it would also serve as his desk where he would spend hours writing. He took the time to move the cabin layout around until he got it just right.

Once the cabin was staked out to his satisfaction, he began gathering native building materials from around the property. He assembled piles of rocks with which to build the foundation, floor, fireplace, and steps. Next, he cut logs for the cabin and outbuildings. He even cut small trees from which to build much of his cabin furniture. The metal roof was recycled from an old barn on the farm. It took David several months to build the cabin himself but it was a labor of love, and the finished cabin showed it. In one end of the cabin where he planned to have his sitting area, library, and couch, he had planned to build a rock fireplace. David knew the fireplace would never heat the 720-square-foot room, so he installed a central wood-burning stove. The opposite end of the cabin was the cooking and sleeping area. Much of his cooking is done on a standard-size gas kitchen stove,

David Brock's one-room Appalachian-style cabin was built from logs and stone found on the site.                                        Photo by JWF

While simple, David Brock's cabin proved to be most comfortable year-round.
                                        Photo by JWF

which uses propane gas. His dining table under double windows indeed enjoys the outstanding view he envisioned having. David elected not to put a front porch across the entire front of his cabin, just enough porch to give the door plenty of protection.

My son and I visited David soon after he completed his cabin. I was most impressed. He had built his dream cabin alone using native materials found on the farm. It was a most comfortable cabin yet rustic enough to make you want to take a lot of photos.

The accompanying plan shows a simple one-room cabin design that I have seen a lot in the Ozarks and the southern Appalachian mountains. It is small, only about 320 square feet inside, but it works well for two to four people. It is heated with a wood-burning stove and is designed to be self-sufficient. Eight-foot porches on the front and back give a lot of covered space outside to eat, take care of equipment, visit, or store gear. It is a fast and easy cabin to build and lends itself well to remote locations. I visited one in Virginia that was three miles from the nearest road, but the builders got the building materials to the site with a four-wheel-drive pickup truck. The owner spent a year living in the little cabin and loved it.

Appalachian Style Cabin
One-room

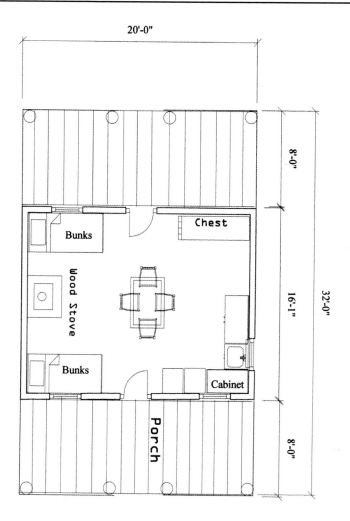

**FRONT**

Floor plan for a one-room Appalachian-style cabin.

## Advantages of the Appalachian-style cabin:

- The simple square or rectangular design makes building easy.
- This structure can be built as a self-sufficient or modern cabin with equal ease.
- The large, low porch gives a lot more space for semiprotected outside activities.
- The traditional structure is an efficient use of space.
- This design is good for those who want a fireplace, but heats efficiently with a wood-burning stove.
- In a wooded setting, the design looks like it belongs there.
- It may be built of logs, plywood, board-and-batten or reverse board-and-batten and they all look good.
- It is one of the more inexpensive cabin designs.

CHAPTER

7

# The Family-Size Cabin

F amily-size cabin means different things to different people. Most people think of multi-bedroom cabins. I can understand that, but before we discuss the larger cabins, let me give you my views on the value of a smaller, self-sufficient cabin.

When my children were growing up, we spent a lot of time together in backcountry cabins due to me being a wildlife professional. Usually these cabins were self-sufficient cabins with only one or two rooms. There were no outside interferences like TV or boom boxes, just us working and playing together in nature. As a result of these "primitive" cabin adventures the kids learned new skills, how to work as a team, and how to live with nature and not try to change nature. We were close, and thanks to those days, we are close now. Those days are some of our fondest memories.

Now my grandchildren are reaching the cabin living age, and we are getting to know one another at my Cross Creek Hollow cabin. I have to admit that we went through a stage when they asked where the light switch was, or where was the TV, but we have gotten over that and moved on to much greater adventures. To them the cabin is in the heart of wilderness, a grand adventure, and they have caught on to the fact that we must do certain things if we are to live comfortably. Now they know when to replenish the firewood box, or go to the creek for water to wash dishes, or sweep the outhouse. They are learning such skills as how to start a fire safely, how to plant food plots for wildlife, how to clean fish, and how to cook in Dutch ovens. They are experiencing a lifestyle that, at least for a short time, is not tied to a clock, a phone, or a computer. They love coming to the cabin, and their friends stand in line for an invitation. Without the cabin, we would miss out on all this.

Having only two rooms in our cabin is an asset, and we do not miss a larger cabin. We enjoy each other's company and spend valuable time discussing things important in their young lives that we would never discuss if they were in another room watching TV or on the phone. Times spent sitting on the porch watching wild turkey feed or sitting in front of the stove talking about what bothers them are special times. We are best friends and the two rooms works just fine for us.

## Larger Cabins for Families

For other families, a larger cabin may enhance the good times. Many times modern conveniences like indoor plumbing, hot and cold running water, and electricity are desired in order to cut down on the workload and to give everyone more time for outdoor recreation and relaxing together. Also, families want more than one bedroom if the parents stay up later or arise earlier than the children. There may be a need for more room if there are small

Family-size cabins are usually larger with multiple bedrooms. This Maine cabin can comfortably accommodate six people.                    Photo by JWF

children in the cabin for long periods during inclement weather. If you often have overnight guests here is another reason for having more than one bedroom. Simply put, a one-room cabin is not for everyone.

There are cabins, both in the Alaskan trapper's–style design and the Appalachian-style design, which meet these needs without breaking the budget. They can be built with modern conveniences or as self-sufficient cabins. The choice is yours.

## ONE BEDROOM WITH SLEEPING LOFT

One of the most efficient family-size cabins I have ever built is a one-bedroom cabin with a large sleeping loft over the bedroom and bathroom. It has stairs going up to the sleeping loft from the great room. This cabin floor plan is very versatile, as it can be built from logs, board-and-batten plywood, or reverse board-and-batten. Also, it can be of the Alaskan trapper's–style design or the Appalachian-style design, depending upon which roof and porch design you use. The one I built was the Appalachian-style, as I wanted a large screened-in back porch for sleeping during the summer.

This is 22 feet 6 inches by 30 feet 6 inches, outside dimensions. If you add both an 8-foot front and back porch, as I did, the dimensions will be 38 feet 6 inches by 30 feet 6 inches. The great room has a cathedral ceiling and is large, 17 feet by 21 feet 10 inches, including the kitchen and dining area. There is a coat closet under the stairs and a small enclosed yet accessible area for the hot water heater. The bedroom is 12 feet by 14 feet 3 inches and convenient to the modern bathroom. It also has a large walk-in closet. The sleeping loft can accommodate four twin-size beds and has a railing along the edge overlooking the great room.

This cabin is designed for central heating and air conditioning. Neither of these would be necessary in cooler climates, however, with a wood-burning stove in the great room and ceiling fans in each room.

My good friends Ken and Pam French have a modern Alaskan trapper's–style cabin with a version of this floor plan on a lake near Millinocket, Maine. It is heated with a wood-burning stove and does not need air conditioning. They enclosed the sleeping loft, complete with a door, and made it a private bedroom. I have stayed there in different seasons of the year and found it to be most comfortable.

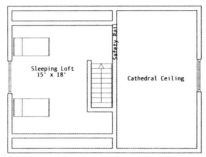

Two-story family size cabin with one bedroom and sleeping loft

**Second Floor**

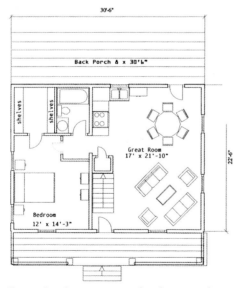

Floor plan for two-story family-size cabin.

Large family-size cabin
front

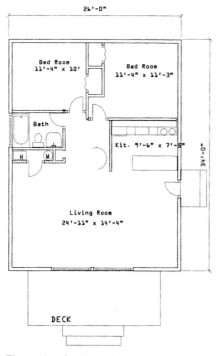

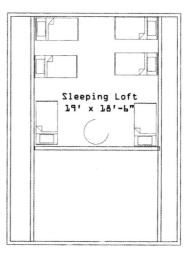

Floor plan for large family-size cabin.

## LARGE FAMILY CABIN

A floor plan that meets the needs of a larger family or a family that has company frequently is one that combines the sleeping space of two downstairs bedrooms and a large sleeping loft upstairs. Just like the smaller one-bedroom family cabin, this one can be built from a variety of materials and can be either an Alaskan trapper's–style or an Appalachian-style, depending upon your choice of treatments of the porch.

The first level of this 26-by-24-foot floor plan contains 880 square feet of floor space, and the sleeping loft adds another 500 square feet. Circular stairs, to save room, connect the two levels. The main floor features a great room, a kitchen, a bathroom, and two 11-by-11-foot bedrooms. The sleeping loft has enough room for six twin-size beds.

A large fireplace insert stove can heat this cabin; however, this floor plan lends itself to central heating and air conditioning if desired.

There is a great selection of family-size cabins offered by many of the log home companies. These cabins may be purchased as kits and built on your site.

Large or small, a cabin can be a special place for a family, and the cost can be a wonderful investment in helping hold a family together.

# The Hunting/Fishing Club Cabin

No one knows for sure, but there may be more cabins being built today for hunting and fishing groups/clubs than for any other purpose. As hunting and fishing lands grow more limited, and as lakefront property on good fishing lakes becomes less available and affordable, there has been a rapid growth in the number of hunting and fishing clubs leasing land on a long-term basis, and this has given rise to an increase in the numbers of cabins being built by these groups. In some cases the lessor will build a cabin for the lessee if the lease is for a long enough period. In other cases, the lessees will pool their financial resources and building skills to build their own cabin. In either case, the cabin becomes the center of the activity and often a home away from home for the members.

Cabins for hunting and fishing clubs are usually economical to construct, as one large bedroom will sleep the members, showers replace bathtubs in the bathroom, and the great room can usually include the kitchen.

Whatever the design, I would suggest that when a cabin is intended for a hunting club or any group where shooting sports are enjoyed, that a lockable gun room be incorporated in the floor plan. Members should be required to place their guns, unloaded, into the gun rack in the gun room until ready for the next outing. I know of several accidents at club cabins where guns were placed in bedrooms or great rooms. A closet can be made into a gun room easily.

## APPALACHIAN-STYLE HUNTING/FISHING CABIN

Back in the 1980s I built a 10-man hunting cabin named "Warrior Lodge" that stands in good shape today after years of hard use. The same group has used the cabin all these years and likes the design. It is not difficult or expensive to build, and is designed for low maintenance. The cabin itself measures 28 by 36 feet, giving 1,008 square feet of living space. A large front porch, 8 feet wide, gives lots of protected outdoor space for visiting or cleaning equipment.

I used reverse board-and-batten siding but logs, plywood, board-and-batten, or log siding would work just as well. To stand up to the hard use I knew it would get, the cabin has a concrete floor with tiles as a floor covering, and the interior walls are reverse board-and-batten.

The site I chose for the cabin, while far from any other houses, has good road access, electrical and telephone service, and a county water system.

The great room is 18 feet by 21 feet 6 inches and has a fireplace. A 9 feet 6 inches by 13 feet 6 inches kitchen joins the great room on the back. The kitchen is modern with electric range and oven, refrigerator, and stainless steel sink. The bathroom has a large shower and an extra large hot water heater. The 13-foot-6-inches-by-27-foot bunkroom was designed to accommodate five large bunk beds.

## SELF-SUFFICIENT HUNTING/FISHING CABIN

Many hunting and fishing cabins are far removed from modern utilities. These cabins usually have water brought in, an outhouse out back, camp stoves for cooking, and lanterns for light. Some of my fondest memories are from days and nights I have spent in these primitive cabins. Here men pitched in to get the camp chores done and to spend time in front of a wood-burning stove, reliving adventures of the past.

One of my favorite designs of this type cabin is one that has a large concrete, floored porch with a built-in fireplace for sheltered outdoor cooking. Most activities took place on the porch of this cabin, even in cold weather.

The cabin is 40 feet long with an additional 12-foot porch, and is 16 feet wide. The great room is 16 feet by 24 feet and contains a kitchen area and a large sitting area around a wood-burning stove. The bunkroom is 16 feet squared, and can accommodate six bunk beds. If more room is needed

Hunting/fishing club cabin

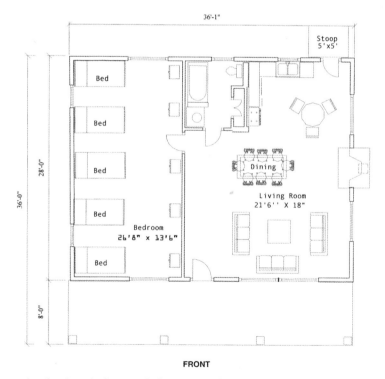

**FRONT**

Floor plan for Appalachian-style hunting or fishing cabin.

Hunting/fishing club cabin

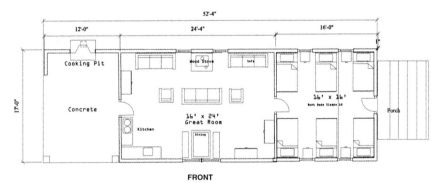

FRONT

Floor plan for self-sufficient hunting/fishing cabin.

this room can be easily enlarged. A door at the end of the bunkroom opens onto a small porch. The cabin was built on a concrete slab. The exterior walls are board-and-batten and the interior walls reverse board-and-batten. The cabin has a metal roof.

Many of these cabins are wired for electricity and a generator furnishes power. In addition, some cabins of this style have a large plastic water reservoir elevated behind the cabin and treated water is brought in to fill the reservoir. Gravity feeds the water to the cabin.

If the cabin has good road access, a large propane tank can be installed and the cabin's lighting, cooking, and heating done with gas.

## Individual Cabins with Group Center

As I was writing this book, I visited a hunting camp in Missouri where members each had a small one-room Appalachian-style cabin to sleep in. For cooking and visiting, there was a large centrally located cabin that contained a great room with fireplace, kitchen/dining room, and shower room. Each night the group would gather in the central cabin for dinner and the telling of tales. Following this they had the privacy of their smaller cabins. This is an interesting concept and must appeal to many, as the club has a waiting list for future memberships.

## Log Cabin Kit for Hunting/Fishing Groups

One log home company, Honest Abe Log Homes, Inc., that has recognized the need for club-size cabins offers an 889-square-foot Alaskan trapper's–style cabin that sleeps six comfortably in the lower level and six in the loft area upstairs. Called the Outpost, this cabin has room for a modern kitchen and bathroom. There is a large sitting area and a large front porch.

Field & Stream Sportsman's Camp by Northeastern Log Homes.

Another company offering a cabin to this market is Northeastern Log Homes, Inc. They have a 1,000-square-foot model called the Field & Stream Sportsman's Camp. This model has plenty of room for a modern kitchen, a bathroom, a great room, and two sleeping lofts. The kit, which costs $22,300 at this writing, includes precut logs, framing lumber, decking, roofing materials, windows, and doors. It is just about all you need to build the cabin except the foundation.

# CHAPTER 9

# Building with Log Cabin Kits/Packages

A t last, you have saved enough money to build your dream cabin, have the perfect site, and have decided that you want a real log cabin. What you don't have are trees on your property that would make good building logs, logging skills, or the time to wait for green logs to season. In addition, you have never notched logs or worked with them to make them fit as walls or around windows and doors. What do you do?

The answer to this question is easy: Shop the many log home companies that offer log cabin kits and select a design that fits your needs and budget. Today there are a lot of good cabin kits available that supply you with most of the building materials you will need to build your cabin and professional assistance to help you get it built right.

## Advantages of Log Cabin Kits

There are many advantages to building your log cabin from a kit. Chief among them is the fact that most log home companies have the experience and equipment to produce a log that will give a lifetime of trouble-free service. Due to modern building-log technology, much of the warping, checking, settling, and splitting of home-cut logs is milled out of the kit logs. All logs are cut to exact size and notching is done in a precise manner. Many log cabin kits are temporarily erected at the company to make sure all fitting is correct. Then the logs are marked, so that the builders will know where each log goes, and taken down for delivery to the new owner.

Log home kits are precision-made structures that arrive on the builder's site
ready to erect.                                                    Photo by JWF

Log home kits vary in what comes with the kit. Some are just the logs; others
are virtually a complete cabin.                                   Photo by JWF

Most log cabin kit companies can supply as much or as little of the other building materials needed to construct the cabin as the new owner wants. These complete packages can be a good buy, as the company knows from experience the best materials to use in completing the cabin. When these materials, such as windows, doors, and trim, are purchased as a part of the package, savings can be passed on to the owner.

Perhaps one of the best parts of a log cabin purchased as a kit is the professional construction consulting made available by the company as you build your cabin. Having someone who has built log cabins many times, from the same type of logs you are using can be a valuable service.

Several years ago I wanted to build a large hunting lodge from logs. I debated whether to go it alone and cut my own logs or to use a log home kit. I elected to purchase a log home kit, and after building the lodge, I was thankful I made that decision. Having logs the right size, length, and that fit where they were supposed to turned out to be more important than I could have guessed. In addition, having an engineer from the log home company available to answer my many questions saved me many hours and much money.

## Disadvantages of Log Cabin Kits

Provided you are dealing with a reputable log home company, there are few disadvantages to purchasing a pre-cut log cabin. Cost is the main disadvantage that some log cabin builders point out. Granted, log cabin kits are not cheap, but when you consider what you get for your money, they are not really expensive. Consider that the pre-cut log cabin is ready to be constructed when it arrives. Most of the building only requires the usual building skills. The kit goes up in a hurry. This saves a lot of time, and time is worth a lot. In addition, the log kit goes up right the first time. What is that worth to you? Considering the log cabin is a lifetime investment, buying a quality kit can be money well spent.

Some cabin builders want the experience of building their log cabin from scratch and consider the log cabin kit to take away from the experience. Anyone who has the time, patience, and resources to build their log cabin from native materials should do it. I would not take anything for the experiences I have had building log cabins in the backcountry. This should not be considered a disadvantage aimed at log cabin kits, but simply a choice.

## CHOOSING A LOG CABIN KIT COMPANY

Today with the popularity of log homes and cabins, there are many log cabin kit companies to choose from. Those listed in appendix 1 of this book name a few offering cabin kits. Any log home magazine will have dozens of advertisements from these companies, mostly promoting log homes. Finding a company is easy, but finding one that specializes in cabins is not.

I have heard some horror stories from people who bought log cabin kits from fly-by-night companies that had little or no experience in log construction. In addition, I have known some folks who negotiated a log cabin kit from a company that made log homes but was not set up to make smaller log cabins. The cabins did not go together as they should have, and the company really didn't want to expand its line into small buildings.

Once you have decided to go with a log cabin kit, contact a number of log home companies and ask for their brochures. Many log home companies sell a planning book and video, both very helpful for learning how to build a log structure from a kit. If the company is serious about the log cabin business, it will have a division devoted to log cabins.

Study the brochures and the options you have available. You may have to choose from several log designs, flooring and roofing may be a part of the package, as may windows and doors. Study the floor plans the company offers. They may have just the plan for you or you may want to design your own and work with your selected company to custom make your cabin.

Ask each company to send you references of log cabin customers within driving distance of where you live. If you really like a particular design and floor plan, ask for references of people who built that cabin. If you are considering a custom cabin, ask for references of those who have built custom cabins using the company's products and services. Next, go visit these customers and look at their cabins. Go with a list of questions:

- Do they like their cabin?
- What do they dislike about the cabin?
- How much did the kit cost and what did it include?
- What did it cost to have the kit delivered, and what part of the unloading did they have to do?
- How long did it take to build the cabin? Were the instructions well written?

- Did the company give good assistance after the sale and during construction?
- What surprises did they experience while building the cabin?
- Would they deal with the company again?
- Also, if you are dealing with a company's local representative, be sure to ask the customers you are visiting about the rep's handling of the cabin purchase and construction support. Many companies have regional representatives to handle the details of the sale. While the company may be a good company, occasionally a bad rep sneaks in, and you don't want to be the one to deal with him.

Be sure to talk to several customers of the company so you can get different perspectives. Talk to only one, and you may be talking to the brother-in-law of the owner.

Look for companies with national reputations, that have been in business for years, and that take cabins just as seriously as they do large homes. It has been my experience that they will treat you right.


## HOW MUCH DOES A KIT COST?

You can pay a little or a lot for a log cabin kit, depending upon what you want. What if you consider a cabin to be a 1500-square-foot, three bedroom, two-bath structure? It will obviously cost a lot more than a 450-square-foot one-room structure. Be reasonable about what you think is a cabin. I consider a cabin to be a structure of not more than about 1,000 square feet.

The price will also depend on what other building materials you want in the kit other than logs, and their quality. A log cabin kit may be reasonably priced, but if you change the windows furnished to double-paned windows and the flooring to high-grade hardwood flooring, the price of the package is going to reflect it.

A big surprise to some log cabin kit purchasers is the cost to ship the log kit to the construction site. Be sure you know what the shipping and handling costs are before you close the deal. Also be aware that you will probably be responsible for unloading the kit and if the delivery truck, often an 18-wheeler, can't get to the building site you will have to get the materials there yourself. This can be a sizable job in the backcountry.

Delivering a log cabin to the construction site may be expensive, and the new owner may be responsible for unloading the truck.

Photo Courtesy Northeastern Log Homes

While site work is not part of pricing a kit, you need to be aware early in the game that the cost of the log cabin kit is only a part of what the finished cabin will cost. Site preparation, getting power to the site, building the foundation, unloading the kit and getting it to the site, hiring construction labor and skilled craftsmen, and purchasing additional building materials and fixtures to finish the interior, all go into the price of the cabin, along with your own sweat equity. The kit cost is just the beginning. How much of the work you and friends can do will have an influence on what the final cost turns out to be.

The cost of a log cabin kit when I was writing this book varied from a low of $4,800 to as much as $28,500, depending upon the contents of the kit or "package," as some log home dealers refer to it. Cost to turn the kit into a finished log cabin depends upon what is included in the kit, but most log home builders I talked with said to be on the safe side, double the cost of the kit to budget the cost of the finished cabin. The log home company you deal with can give you a good estimate based on which kit you want.

## What a Kit/Package May Include

The kit components may vary with different companies, but you need to know what a good kit includes, as this will help you when shopping for companies to consider doing business with. The following sample lists the components of a standard cabin package from Northeastern Log Homes, Inc., one of the leading companies in log home production, with a camp and cabin department. This is the standard materials package that comes with their cabin kits.

## Floor System

- Sills: pressure-treated 2-by-6 inch
- Girders: 2-by-8 inch built up on job
- Headers: 2-by-8-inch spruce
- Floor joists: 2-by-8-inch spruce, 16 inches O.C.
- Floor joist hangers
- Metal cross-bridging
- Subfloor: ⅝-inch tongue-and-groove OSB (Oriented Strand Board) Sturdi-Floor
- Porch and deck floor joists, sills, and headers: 2-by-6-inch PTSYP (Pressure-treated Southern yellow pine)
- Porch and deck flooring: ¾-by-6-inch radiused-edge
- Porch posts

## Log Wall System

- Milled 6-by-8-inch tongue-and-groove pre-cut and numbered wall and gable logs, Eastern white pine
- Camp and Cabin (traditional grade) logs have imperfections and a more rustic look
- All necessary foam gaskets, Puttylastic caulking sealant, pre-compressed corner pads, and 12-inch spiral steel spikes
- Window and door jambs: specially shaped 4-by-4-inch pine with 8-inch spikes
- Milled shiplap log siding as necessary for floor frame skirting, Eastern white pine

- Wall braces: with hardware
- Specially milled 6-by-6-inch splinted posts as required

# Ceiling

- Ceiling joists: 2-by-8-inch spruce 16-inches O.C.
- Ceiling joist hangers
- Metal cross-bridging
- Floor: ⅞-inch tongue-and-groove OSB Sturdi-Floor
- Posts and beams as required

# Roof System

- Rafters: 2-by-6-inch or 2-by-8-inch spruce 16-inches O.C. as required (LVL ridge beams as required)
- Roof support posts with post caps
- Roof sheathing: ⅞-inch tongue-and-groove OSB
- Fascia: 1-by-8-inch D4S pine or 1-by-10-inch D4S pine as required
- Soffits: ¾-inch tongue-and-groove knotty pine boards
- Tarpaper: #15 roofing felt
- Drip edge: 8-inch galvanized drip edge for eaves and rakes
- Shingles: Owens Corning three-tab fiberglass (25-year warranty)
- Porch rafters: 2-by-6-inch spruce 16-inches O.C.
- 6-by-8-inch porch beam
- Roof vents
- Metal connectors for all rafters

# Windows and Doors

- Standard windows are Andersen Builder's Select insulating glass, double-hung with full screens
- Exterior doors: 3 feet by 6 feet, 8 inches pre-hung Therma-Tru premium steel door system
- Exterior window and door trim: random length pine 1⁷⁄₁₆-inches by 3½-inch radius edges
- Schlage exterior lock set
- Backer rod

Please note that not all log cabin kits are as complete as this one while other packages can be truly complete, turnkey jobs. Be sure to get a listing of log cabin kit components from the dealer you are shopping with, and make sure the list is for the kit model you are interested in.

Having looked over the Northeastern log cabin package, you can see that it's fairly complete, and at a cost that would run you a lot more if you had to chase down all the materials yourself. For those who can afford the cost, and whose time for building is limited, the kit is the way to go.

## DESIGNS AND FLOOR PLANS OF SOME POPULAR LOG CABIN KITS

When you look at the cabin offerings of the log home companies, you'll find there are a lot of floor plan options. It would be impossible to discuss them all here, plus the companies add and drop designs periodically. Also you must remember that most floor plans are just suggestions made by the company, as in most cases the interior walls, interior doors, cabinets, plumbing fixtures, etc. are not included in the kit. If you like the cabin exterior but don't like the company's suggested floor plan, you can design your own interior. I include here a selection of kits that lend themselves to being either a self-sufficient or modern cabin with the company's suggested floor plan. The appendix will tell you how to get in touch with the companies.

As I stated above, Northeastern Log Homes, Inc. (Kenduskeag, Maine) has an excellent selection of log cabins. One of their Appalachian-style models I like is the one-bedroom Eagle's Nest. It measures 24 by 28 feet, not counting an 8-foot front porch. Inside, the all-in-one kitchen/living room, combined with full-beamed ceiling and a centrally located wood-burning stove and hearth, make it great for weekend getaways. It has a large bathroom with ample space for a laundry center. The bedroom measures 11 by 12 feet and has a closet. With a total of 672 square feet, this is a well-designed cabin.

For a family-size cabin, Northeastern has two good two-bedroom examples in both the Alaskan trapper's–style cabin and the Appalachian-style cabins. The 24-by-28-foot Alaskan trapper's–style cabin is called the Retreat, with a total of 672 square feet, not including the 8-foot front porch. The living/dining area spreads out to the kitchen for added space efficiency.

The other family-size cabin is the 768-square-foot Rockwood, measuring 24 by 32 feet plus the 8-foot front porch. It features a large living/

The one-bedroom Eagle's Nest, by Northeastern Log Homes.

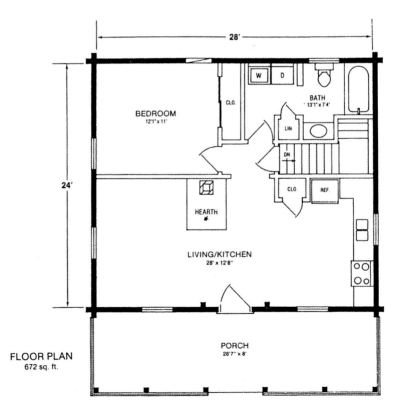

The two-bedroom Retreat, by Northeastern Log Homes.

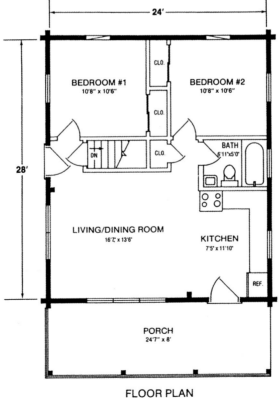

**FLOOR PLAN**
672 sq. ft.

The two-bedroom Rockwood, by Northeastern Log Homes.

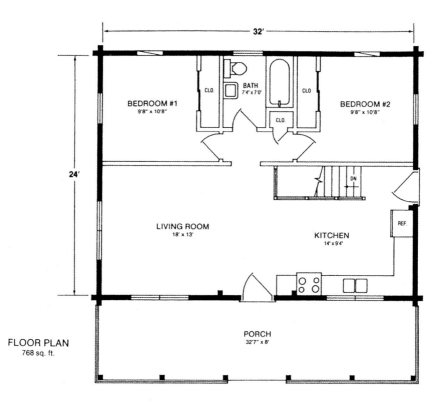

FLOOR PLAN
768 sq. ft.

dining/kitchen area, and a good-sized bathroom conveniently located between the two bedrooms.

At this writing, Northeastern's cabin kit prices from range from $9,700 to $18,400.

Jim Barna Log Systems (Oneida, Tennessee) offers the Harrison, a 416-square-foot Alaskan trapper's–style cabin. This is a one-room log cabin with enough room for a bathroom. It is designed for a fireplace and has a front porch. This would be a great little cabin to build in the heart of hunting and fishing country.

If you want a cabin with the traditional Appalachian-style look, consider the squared-log cabin called the Creekside, made by Suwannee River Log Homes (Wellborn, Florida). This 18-by-24-foot cabin has 432 square feet in the downstairs floor plan with enough room for great room, bathroom, and kitchen/dining room. The great room has a fireplace. The 252-square-foot sleeping loft measures 13-by-17-feet. The cabin has an 8-foot front porch, and it would be easy to add a back porch.

One of the best-known log home companies, Heritage Log Homes (Sevierville, Tennessee) has an attractive family-size cabin called the Banner Elk. This contains 544 square feet of living space. Besides two bedrooms and

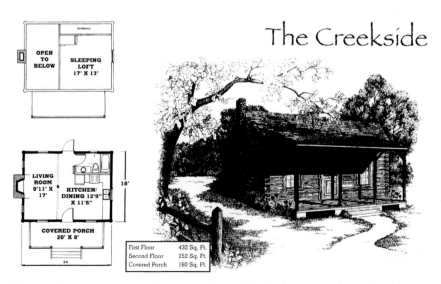

The one-bedroom Appalachian-style Creekside, by Suwannee River Log Homes.

bath, it has a living room and kitchen/dining room. At this writing, the cost of the basic kit is $18,600.

A versatile Appalachian-style log cabin kit is the Mountaineer, made by Honest Abe Log Homes (Moss, Tennessee). It has approximately 560 square feet of floor space and an 8-foot front porch. The floor plan calls for two bedrooms plus a large living room, bathroom, and a kitchen. This would make an ideal family-size cabin.

Kuhns Brothers Log Homes (Lewisburg, PA) has an entire division, called Country Log Cabins, devoted to small log cabins. They are made from 6-by-8-inch kiln dried logs and made to the same standards as the company's well-known log homes. Depending upon your wishes, this company can handle all of your cabin needs from cabin selection, custom design if necessary, to complete construction if desired. Their web site contains a wide selection of floor plans and elevations to help you with your cabin planning.

Another well-known log home company that has a cabin series is Ward Log Homes (Houlton, MA). At this writing, they offer four cabins ranging in size from 160 square feet to 600 square feet.

## LOG PANEL KITS

If you want a small cabin fast, I would suggest you take a look at the cabins offered by Panel Concepts Inc. (Mio, Michigan) These cabins are of the Alaskan trapper's style and are available in sizes from 12 by 12 feet to 20 by 40 feet. Their panel construction makes these cabin kits easy to transport to remote locations, fast and easy to put together plus they can be disassembled and moved easily if necessary.

All of the company's cabin kits come in panels, and every component is a part of a panel to eliminate pieces and labor cost. When the company makes a wall panel, each log (kiln dried red or white pine) has a double tongue and groove milled on top and bottom. The outer surface is milled round like a log, and the inside surface is milled to look like knotty pine paneling. When the panels are assembled, expandable foam is sprayed between the tongues of each log to seal out the weather. Each wall panel is 4 feet wide by 7 feet, 7 inches long.

The panels are easily assembled with screws to make walls in 4-foot increments to the cabin's desired dimensions. Any type of floor system may be used with the panels. The roof is also made in panels for ease of construc-

Panel Concepts, Inc. cabin kits are shipped as panels, and the cabin can be put up in one to two days.

tion. Inside, the panels give the look of an open beam ceiling with knotty pine decking.

Assembly of the building is a simple and unique system. Each panel is fastened to another with high-grade screws, which have a special coating to prevent rust and corrosion. Each wall panel is numbered to correspond with a diagram in the instructions. The roof panels are all the same to prevent confusion during assembly. The complete building can be assembled with a ladder, screw gun, a level, a hammer, and a chalk line. For some cabins, the doors and windows are installed in the panels at the factory.

If the cabin needs to be moved after construction, it is a simple matter of removing the screws and disassembling the shell. The panels may be fastened together and reassembled after being moved to the new location.

The 16-by-20-foot AuSable Country cabin kit, featuring 2-by-8-inch rafters and 3½-inch foam insulation in the roof, makes a nice one-room cabin. The $^{12}\!/_{12}$-pitch roof is engineered for a 117-pound-per-square-inch snow load and allowing a 12-inch overhang on the sides and back of the

The AuSable Country Cabin is made from a log panel kit by Panel Concepts, Inc.

cabin. There is an attractive 8-by-16-foot covered front porch. The interior walls are 7 feet, 8 inches high, and the ceiling at the peak is 15 feet, 8 inches. At this writing, this kit sells for $14,128 plus shipping from Mio, Michigan.

The kit includes wall panels, a 36-inch wooden door, insulated roof panels, three single-hung aluminum windows, screens, and all fasteners.

## LOG SIDING KITS

There are log siding cabin kits available as well. EZ Home Kits (Audubon, Pennsylvania) offers a wide selection of log siding kits with a variety of floor plans and exterior designs. Many of their kits contain more than just exterior building materials. This is a web site worth visiting if you are interested in building with log siding.

All of the kit companies I talked to while researching this book told me the demand for small cabins was growing rapidly, and that they were expanding their offerings in cabins that lend themselves to being self-sufficient or modern.

If you are interested in log cabin kits, be sure to visit the web site that serves as a log home directory—www.lhoti.com. You can find almost anything on log homes or cabins you are looking for.

# 10

# The World's Best Outhouse

The remote cabin may not have running water, and if not that rules out the modern bathroom. Usually the next best option is an outhouse, or privy, as some prefer to call the little house out back.

During the 30-plus years of my outdoor career, I have had firsthand experience with outhouses throughout much of the world, and most of it has not been very pleasant. I have seen very few outhouses I liked. When I decided to build my Cross Creek Hollow cabin, I decided that I would build an outhouse that would always be clean, bright, insect-free, odorless, and roomy enough for the visit to be pleasant, even for the visitor who had never seen such a restroom.

As I was researching the perfect outhouse plan, I read in a newspaper that the U.S. Forest Service had a new plan for odor-free privies, and that they were going to rework all of their outhouses. It occurred to me that they should know, as they were at that time the manager of 12,000 outhouses in our national forest, and they build about 300 new ones each year. The development of the odor-free outhouse was done at the Forest Service research lab in California. I got in contact with them and used their research for designing, building, and managing my outhouse. I also obtained some useful outhouse design tips from several missionary groups who were helping remote villages in Central America build outhouses that are more sanitary.

## Building Cross Creek Hollow's Outhouse

My first step in building the outhouse was to check with my county health department to see that it was permissible. It was, so long as it was well away

The Cross Creek Hollow outhouse is located over 100 feet from the cabin, and downwind.                                                    Photo by JWF

from any water supply such as a well or spring, and it didn't require a permit. The site I selected for the outhouse was 100 feet from the cabin and downwind from the prevailing wind. There was no water source anywhere near the privy, and the water table was known to be many feet lower than the bottom of the pit. It would be convenient to the cabin, and I positioned the front door so there would be a good view from the inside looking out with the door open. The 57-by-60-inch building was staked out, and I was ready to start to work.

First, I dug a 48-by-48-inch square pit, 5 feet deep. To shore up the pit, I built a boxlike structure from pressure-treated lumber, just a simple box of 1-by-8-by-48-inch boards spaced 2 inches apart, screwed into a 2-by-4 in each corner. There is no bottom or top. The box was pushed down into the pit with the top level with the floor of the outhouse. Its role is to keep the sides of the pit from caving in over time.

On top of this, I framed-in the outhouse floor using pressure-treated framing and ¾-inch marine plywood. Since I was using a purchased seat assembly for the actual "throne," I had to make sure the floor joists were spaced to allow for the opening in the floor. Also, before installing the walls it was important to mark the opening needed for the seat assembly and cut out the floor with a saber saw. I cut the opening in the floor for the vent pipe at the same time. Cutting these holes after the walls went up would be difficult.

With the floor in place, the framing went up quickly. I finished the walls with log siding to match the cabin. At the top of each sidewall, I cut a vent opening and installed hardware cloth to keep insects from coming in

Cross Creek Hollow's outhouse is built with log siding to match the cabin and has a translucent roof to let in light.                    Photo by JWF

through the vents. For roofing, I used translucent fiberglass so the outhouse would be bright during the day. I cut a hole in the roof and pushed a 6-inch PVC sewer drainpipe down from the roof into the floor to serve as a pit vent pipe, leaving it higher than the roof to ensure good ventilation. The pipe, held in place with pipe strapping, was painted black above the roof so it would collect solar heat and pull air from the pit.

Following this, I installed the floor covering, a light-colored linoleum that would be easy to clean and give the floor a tight seal. After cutting a

The interior of the author's outhouse is bright and clean and features a stainless-steel seat.                                    Photo by JWF

hole in the floor covering, I installed the stainless steel seat assembly. Finally, I built a homemade door from 1-by-6-inch boards, and painted a quarter moon on the finished door to keep with tradition.

I painted the inside walls with an off-white enamel to brighten the interior, and mounted a battery-operated light on the wall, a toilet paper dispenser, within easy reach. A container of builder's lime sits next to the seat. As a finishing touch, I added some pictures to the walls.

## MAINTAINING THE OUTHOUSE

It is a requirement that a cup of builder's lime be thrown in the pit after each use of the toilet. This is our method of flushing. Also, I ask that the seat lid be kept shut so that the gases will go out the vent pipe and not into the building, and it keeps any insects from getting into the building. Twice each year I pour a solution of one package of yeast in one quart of warm water into the pit. The fermentation breaks down the deposits. I have a strict rule that no other waste, such as garbage, is thrown into the pit. I have seen many outhouses be ruined when they were used as a garbage dump. Use it for only what it was designed for. Some outhouse owners I know take one can of common household lye and shake it down in the pit once a month to eat away the waste. I have never tried this, as the method I use works great. In fact, my outhouse has been used for over ten years without any problems or getting too full.

Hanging inside the outhouse is a broom for cleaning. On a shelf is extra toilet tissue and air freshener. On the outside of the outhouse next to the steps is a solar-powered light that shows the way to the building from the cabin at night.

My outhouse is not insulated, as we do not need it in the South, but in colder climates, it would be easy to insulate the building. We do have a Styrofoam seat cover for cold mornings.

For really cold days, I put a Coleman BlackCat catalytic heater in the outhouse. This heater is designed for use in enclosed areas and uses a 16.4-ounce propane cylinder as a fuel source. It features flameless platinum catalytic technology and has an 8-inch heating head. It is rated for 3,000 BTU output. It will take the chill out of a cold outhouse in just a few minutes.

I have also posted the rules for using the outhouse and the cabin on the door at eye level when sitting on the seat. It just reminds us all of how the property is to be taken care of.

- Always keep the door closed unless you are enjoying the view during the visit.
- Keep the toilet lid closed when not in use.
- Use a cup of lime after depositing waste in the pit.
- Pour in a quart of yeast/warm water once monthly.
- Do not put anything but human waste and toilet paper in the pit. Toilet paper rolls, sanitary napkins, paper towels, cigarette butts, and garbage of any kind goes into the cabin trash.
- Clean out the vent pipe twice annually. Spider webs will cause it not to function.
- Clean off the roof twice annually, as leaves will cut out the light.
- Sweep out the outhouse daily.
- Clean the interior walls, toilet seat, and floor every three months with a disinfectant cleaner.
- Spray for insects each May and August.
- Wash your hands in the washbasin on the cabin porch before entering the cabin.

I have found that these rules prevent problems. Many of my guests have never spent time in a self-sufficient cabin before, and you can't expect them to know all these things. I don't think the rules have ever made anyone mad, and our outhouse has been consistently odor-free, clean, bright, and insect-free for years.

## Waterless Composting Toilets

If you want a toilet inside the self-sufficient cabin, or you want to have a state-of-the-art outhouse, then you should consider one of the waterless, self-contained composting toilets. These units require no water, no septic system, no chemicals and they do not smell or pollute. The system is really simple, and uses nature to solve our sewage problem. The unit uses the continuous action of aerobic microbes to reduce waste into reusable compost. Waste material enters the toilet; about 90 percent of it is water. The toilet evaporates most of the water, and the vapors are carried up through the vent pipe and dispersed into the air, odorlessly. Heat, oxygen, and organic material break down the remaining waste into compost. I have seen these units in remote lodges, family-size cabins, oil exploration camps, mines, and native villages throughout the world and when properly used they work great.

There are two units that I have experience with, the Envirolet Basic Plus and the #NE unit sold by Lehman's. Both are non-electric. I will discuss these two units here.

There are several things to like about these units. First, they are self-contained. They are easy to install and come with a vent kit. The Envirolet Basic Plus, made by Sancor, measures 25 inches wide by 33 inches long by 25 inches high (19.75 inches height to toilet seat). It weighs 74 pounds. The Lehman's #NE measures 31 inches high by 22½ inches wide by 33 inches long. (The seat height is 17 inches.) This unit weighs 95 pounds. The Envirolet unit cost $1,175 and the Lehman's $879 at this writing. These units are designed to be used in cabins accommodating three to six people.

The Envirolet composting toilet requires no water, electricity, chemicals, or septic system.

Use of the toilet is simple. A small amount of peat moss is added to the toilet when it is used. Every few days the toilet is agitated and mixed with a built-in mixer, in an odorless process. The compost drops down into a bottom drawer for removal. This is only required every few weeks or less, depending upon use.

One of the real pluses of these units is that they may be used or left unattended in the winter without worrying about freezing up. They work regardless of temperature. These units are made from durable material and are easy to clean.

Both companies offer a variety of models; some larger units work well where electricity is available. These toilets are the closest you can get to a modern toilet in the backcountry where electricity and running water are not possible. They can give you the comfort and convenience of an indoor toilet.

## BURNING HUMAN WASTE

Here is a more expensive method of human waste disposal, but a good one. The propane Storburn toilet, sold by Lehman's, is designed for remote locations. It does not need electricity or running water, so it can be installed about anywhere, even in the coldest regions. It has the capacity to handle eight full-time users or ten part-time users.

It works like an incinerator, treating human waste by burning it, reducing the waste to minerals and water vapor. The burner is fired by propane and is approved by both Canadian and American Gas Associations. It is sanitary, safe (harmful bacteria is destroyed by heat), and non-polluting. Since there are no moving parts or electrical systems, maintenance is simple, just sweep out the ashes.

Operating the burning cycle is easy. Starting the burner is about as easy as lighting a gas grill: add a packet of anti-foam, close the unit, and press a button to light the burner. There is no chance of burning yourself as the unit must be closed and locked before it will burn. Start the cycle before going to bed, and when you wake up the toilet chamber is clean and empty. This toilet, which is known for having no foul odors, sells for $2,650 at this writing, a little expensive, but it is a great way to handle human waste in remote locations.

The Storburn toilet uses propane to burn waste.

## OPTIONS

There are other means of handling human waste in self-sufficient cabins. Some people use portable chemical toilets, but I find these messy to handle and I don't think I have seen one that was used over a long weekend, especially in the summer, that didn't have bad breath. Also, there are some toilets that are simply holding tanks that leave a lot to be desired. I would hate to face a trip home Sunday afternoon from my cabin with a container of human waste in the car.

The modern bathroom is hard to beat, but if you want a self-sufficient cabin in the backcountry, the well-designed outhouse or waterless composting toilet can be almost as good.

# 11

# Keeping the Cabin Warm

As I did the research for this book, I went back and read all the old books I could find on building cabins. Interestingly, most of the authors based their cabin designs around the method that would be used to heat the cabin. Some sang the praises of the fireplace, and in their cabins, the fireplace was the center of activity. Others sang the praises of the wood-burning stove, of one type or another. The one thing that ran common with all of them was that the crackle of a wood-burning fire had a lot to do with the spirit of the cabin. With that, I agree.

There are several advantages to using wood. Wood is a renewable resource and is usually available locally. Environmentalists prefer wood to fossil fuels for heating because of wood's lower sulfur levels. Even the ashes from a wood fire are useful as fertilizer. In addition, wood is usually cheaper to use for heating a cabin. Moreover, as the saying goes, it will heat you twice, once when cutting, splitting, and stacking it, and again when burning it.

I have stayed in cabins that had comfortable and convenient central heating. I have stayed in others that had propane or oil heaters. All of these did a good job of heating the cabin, but something was missing. Gone was the self-sufficient feeling, the independent feeling that comes with a wood-burning fire. Perhaps it is the selecting, cutting, stacking, and seasoning of all that wood during the spring. Perhaps it is the act of getting a good fire going from scratch in the stove or fireplace that brings out something in us that dates back to when man first conquered fire. Maybe it is the smell of wood smoke in the cabin or the sound of hickory or oak crackling in the fire that makes us enjoy the freedom of cabin living. Whatever the reason, I think a getaway cabin should have either a fireplace or a wood-burning stove to complement the backcountry environment we seek. Staying in a cabin on

a cold winter's night without a wood-burning stove or fireplace is an experience that is incomplete.

## FIREPLACE OR STOVE?

When I first started going into the far north, I soon noticed a definite shortage of fireplaces in cabins and lodges. At first, I thought it must be due to
the shortage of bricks, suitable rocks, cement, or knowledgeable masons.
When I got up enough courage to ask, I found that it was the opinion of
most cabin dwellers that fireplaces lost too much heat and stoves were much
more efficient. Indeed, I soon discovered this was true.

According to wood products specialists with the Cooperative Agricul-
ture Extension Service, the fireplace is no match for heating efficiency when
compared to an airtight wood-burning stove. In fact, they state that a fireplace may lose as much as 90 percent of its heat up the chimney, and as it
pushes hot air out of the cabin it pulls cold air into the cabin. According to
reports, the heating efficiency of the airtight wood-burning stove is 60 percent, the fireplace is 10 percent at best. They state, "You can get more heat if

According to experts, the fireplace, though picturesque, is no match for heating
efficiency when compared to an airtight wood-burning stove.    Photo by JWF

you can control the excess air and get a fire and combustion temperature up quicker. A wood-burning stove is far superior to a fireplace because it controls the air admitted to its combustion chamber and it has more radiating surface. The stove makes better use of the heat produced by the wood."

I once built a hunting lodge and had a master mason build a fireplace in the great room. The lodge also had central heating, and it was a good thing. Anytime we built a fire in the fireplace, the great room got cold as the chimney pulled the warm air out of the room faster than the new air being pulled into the room could be heated. It was a beautiful fireplace to look at, but most inefficient for heating.

Tom Walker, a cabin building expert, stated in his book *Building The Alaska Log Home,* that nowhere in his book will the reader find fireplaces or fireplace designs because open fireplaces have no real practical value in a cabin or northern home.

Having said all that if you insist on having a fireplace in your cabin, keep the following in mind:

- Get the best mason you can find with fireplace experience. Get references, and visit past customers to see the quality of his work and the owner's satisfaction with the fireplace.
- Know that the fireplace and chimney are going to be much more expensive than a top-quality wood-burning stove and chimney. At this writing a fireplace and chimney cost from $5,000 to $8,000, depending upon the materials used.
- Make sure the fireplace is designed for the size of the cabin. Too large a fireplace will never heat a room, as it pulls too much air too fast. The smaller fireplace is usually more efficient.
- The top of the chimney should extend up at least 18 inches above the highest point of the cabin roof so it will draw.
- Make sure there are no limbs or trees near the chimney to interfere with the draft.
- All fireplaces should have a damper. Closing the damper cuts off airflow up the chimney when the fireplace is not in use, and keeps out insects, leaves, etc. during the warm months.
- Consider having glass doors installed in the fireplace opening so ´ that they can be closed when you go to bed, both for safety and to keep the cabin from losing valuable heat when the fire goes out.
- Be sure the hearth is large enough to catch sparks and stray embers.

## THE RIGHT WOOD STOVE FOR YOUR CABIN

If you are new to the world of wood-burning stoves, then you are in for a surprise when you start shopping. There are a lot of different designs, types, prices, and sizes of wood-burning stoves. Trying to find the right stove for your cabin can be very confusing, and you will go home with the wrong stove if you don't study the situation carefully and make an informed decision.

Books have been written on how to choose a stove, and I could spend pages in this book discussing the various stoves currently available. However, let's make it simple and consider the important points in selecting a stove for your cabin.

First and foremost, you want the safest stove you can buy. Remember, you are building a fire inside your cabin, and fire destroys more cabins than any other cause. Avoid used stoves that have seen hard use. Often they have cracks and leaks in the firebox you can't see. Avoid cheap stoves with thin walls, doors that do not seal tight, and little or no control of air intake. In short, stay with quality-made brand-name stoves that have a reputation for being safe.

Next, you want a stove that will heat efficiently. The airtight stoves have proven to be the best-designed type for getting the most even heat for the amount of wood burned. Airtight construction means that all joints and seams are sealed, doors are precision-fitted and gasketed. Air inlets are designed and placed to admit a controlled amount of air at the correct point in the combustion process.

You will want a stove with a secondary combustion chamber so that heat is extracted from flue gases and other products of primary combustion before they are drawn off. An internal baffle in the stove circulates these flammable elements back to the fire, where they burn more completely.

For those cold winter nights, you will want a stove that will hold a fire overnight. Most of the airtight stoves, if properly adjusted, will hold a fire overnight. The catalytic stoves will usually hold a fire a little longer.

The size of the stove should be matched to the size of your cabin. This is not a case where bigger is better. There is nothing more uncomfortable and labor intensive than a wood-burning stove too large for the cabin. Conversely, it is most disappointing to try to heat a large cabin with a stove that is not capable of putting out enough BTUs to evenly heat the structure. There is no rule of thumb for stove size. Talk to other cabin owners who have a cabin similar to yours, and see what stove they use. Some stove shops have knowledgeable sales staffs who can help you pick the right size stove, but I would rather ask them for references and talk to people who are using the stove before making a decision.

When shopping for a stove, bear in mind that many things affect the results you are going to get from your stove. The type and dryness of your wood supply, how well your cabin is insulated, how much wood you are burning, and how well your stove is adjusted, all play a role in how warm your cabin will be.

You will be off on the right foot if you shop at stores that carry top quality stoves such as Vermont Castings, Federal, Jotul, Waterford, Hearthstone, and Fisher. If you don't have a stove store near you, purchase the Lehman's catalog (see appendix). They have a huge selection of wood-burning stoves, and their catalog contains a lot of information to help you in deciding on a stove for your cabin.

When I started shopping for a stove for my Cross Creek Hollow cabin, I made up a list of requirements. I had no preconceived idea as to what brand or model stove I wanted. I would buy the one that met my requirements. They were:

- I wanted to heat 300 to 500 square feet of a cabin that had high ceilings.
- I wanted an airtight stove with catalytic combustion for fuel efficiency and clean smoke emissions.
- I wanted a stove with a top I could cook on if I so desired.
- I wanted a stove with front-opening doors and, with a fire screen in place, I could use like a fireplace.
- To make cleaning out ashes easy, I wanted the stove to have an ash drawer.
- The stove had to be made by a well-known stove maker and guaranteed, as it was a long-term investment.

After shopping and comparing, I decided on the small Federal stove. It cost about $800 at that time. The small Federal is 29¾ inches high, 22 inches wide, and 16 inches deep and weighs 380 pounds. It takes 18-inch fire logs and has a burning time of about seven hours. I am told its maximum output is 35,000 BTUs of heat.

The little stove has seen a lot of use since then, and today it works, and looks, as good as new. As with any catalytic-combustion stove you have to replace the combustor every few years, but that is only $90 or so and for the value received, it is money well spent.

The size of the stove should be matched to the size of your cabin. The author selected this Federal airtight stove for his Cross Creek Cabin.    Photo by JWF

Here I should say a few words about catalytic combustion. Catalytic combustion in a wood-burning stove is similar to that what occurs in the motor vehicle. It consists of the after-burning of gases given off by burning wood. When wood burns, certain gasses are given off. These gases are themselves flammable, and are, in fact, a potential source of additional fuel.

Even airtight stoves with their many efficient qualities produce a lot of smoke and creosote. Catalytic combustion burns much of it up. Since as much as one-third of the potential heat in a log can be released as smoke, catalytic combustion results in higher fuel efficiencies. During slow-burning, overnight fires, efficiency can be increased dramatically. Because the smoke is being burned, catalytic combustion reduces smoke pollution, reducing smoke emissions as much as 90 percent. Since creosote, a tar that condenses on the inside of chimneys and can cause deadly chimney fires, is burned in the catalytic combustor stoves, this feature is considered safer.

## LOCATING AND INSTALLING THE STOVE

Regardless of what type of stove you settle on, the correct installation will have a lot to do with its safety and satisfaction.

A good alternative to a fireplace is a modern wood-burning stove which can be opened in the front to expose the fire.                    Photo by JWF

Pick a central location in your cabin to set up your stove. It should be in an area where it won't impede traffic or block exits. Be sure the hearth area allows space for loading the stove and emptying ashes.

Maintain adequate clearance to combustible materials such as furniture, wooden walls, and curtains. The space between the stove and any combustibles should be checked before starting the installation. The instructions for the stove should come with state-recommended clearances.

When building a new cabin you should plan on the location of the stove and build a hearth and protected wall for the stove. Use recommended materials for floor and wall protection. When I built my Cross Creek Hollow cabin, I built a corner in the cabin especially for the stove. A corner of the floor was braced for the stove's additional weight, and thick rock was used for the hearth and wall for protection. The stove clearance was based on the manufacturer's recommendations. This area looks good in the cabin and assures safety from heat and fallen hot coals.

If you are connecting a stove to an existing chimney, the chimney should be checked thoroughly for adequate size, type, and condition. Putting old, unsafe brick and masonry chimneys back into use can be dangerous. Be sure the chimney is sound and has a flue liner.

Building a cabin with a built-in rock hearth assures safety for wood-burning stove use.                                           Photo by JWF

Adjacent to your stove should be space for a fire extinguisher, kindling container, ash bucket, poker, small broom, and other stove attachments. They should be stored neatly and out of the way when not needed.

Here is one last tip on installing wood-burning stoves. When your stove arrives at your cabin, have a lot of help to get it unloaded and placed on the hearth. The last stove I purchased, a very small stove I might add, was loaded inside my pickup truck while I was paying for it. My truck had a camper shell on the back, so it was like putting a stove in a cave. When I arrived at my cabin a friend and I went inside the truck to move the stove out. It didn't move. Later I learned the loaders at the stove shop used a forklift to load it. It took three strong men to get my stove, which now didn't seem so small, out of the truck and properly placed in the cabin.

## STOVEPIPE SELECTION AND INSTALLATION

Selection of your stovepipe and chimney is just as important as choosing your stove. The world's greatest stove with an improper chimney system is dangerous and ineffective. The size of the chimney MUST match the size of the stove collar, because that is the flue size for which your stove was designed and tested. An oversize chimney pulls too much heat into the chimney. An undersize chimney creates too little draft and a smoky burn.

Chimney height is also important. If the chimney is too short to create a stable draft, you get a minimum burn. Very tall chimneys may cause over-drafting. Fire codes require that the top of a chimney must be at least 3 feet above the roof, and at least 2 feet above any part of the cabin within 10 feet.

Simply put, the chimney has two jobs. One is to get rid of smoke. The other is to create the draft that keeps the fire burning.

If the chimney is wrong, the draft is wrong. With too much draft, too much heat is going up the chimney. With too little draft, you get smoky fires that pollute the chimney with dangerous creosote while polluting the air with smoke.

The chimney system I have used on several cabins, with complete satisfaction, is the Dura/Plus fire safe metal chimney. The heart of this system is the two layers of insulation, ceramic blanket, and air space; keeping the chimney cool outside to protect the cabin, and hot inside to boost stove efficiency. The Dura/Plus starter section sits at the bottom of the chimney support box. If a chimney fire does erupt, cool air sweeps into the air space by convection and cools the chimney to protect both chimney and cabin.

## Installing a Dura/Plus Chimney

Perhaps one of the things I liked most about this chimney system was its ease of installation. Even if you elect to use another chimney system, reading the Dura/Plus installation instructions will give you a good idea as to how a quality chimney system should go in. Whatever the system you install, always read the instructions and follow them to the letter.

The first step is planning how much stovepipe you will need, which chimney kit fits your stove, and the number and length of chimney sections you will need. Once you have decided on a stove, your chimney dealer can help you get the right components.

Installation begins with placing the stove in its permanent location. Make sure this is where you want it, because from this point on there's no turning back. Next, drop a plumb line to the center of the stove flue collar. Mark the center point on the ceiling of the cabin. Cut and frame a 14½ inch square opening around the center point.

Slide the chimney support box into the framed opening from below, and level it. Two inches of the box should extend below the ceiling if there is an attic in the cabin. Nail the chimney support box to the framed opening from above with at least two 8-penny nails on each side. Screw the support box trim to the ceiling.

From above, lower the Dura/Plus starter section into the support box. Never substitute a chimney section in place of the starter section. As I stated earlier, this is the heart of this system. Put it in the wrong place, and the system fails.

Now lower the first chimney section over the starter section. Press together and twist to lock in place. Be sure arrows point up. Next, if you are working in an attic, slip the insulation shield over the chimney until the base sits squarely on the frame opening. Nail the shield to the opening with at least two eight-penny nails per side. Wrap the insulation shield collar around chimney and slide it down to the shield.

With this done, you are now ready to cut to the outside. Drop a plumb line from the roof to the center of chimney. This establishes the center point for cutting a round hole through the roof. The hole in the cabin roof must provide at least a 2-inch clearance all around the chimney. Add more chimney sections and twist to lock. Make sure they are level. The remaining installation will take place on the roof.

Slip aluminum flashing over the roof hole, and nail the top edge to the roof under the roofing. Seal the nail heads with mastic. Add more chimney sections until the chimney is at least 3 feet above the roof, and at least 2 feet above any part of the cabin within 10 feet. Apply mastic where storm collar will meet chimney and slide down. Seal with mastic. Add enough chimney sections to meet the height requirements, and snap on the chimney cap.

## STOVE SAFETY

As you use your new stove and chimney, use some common sense. Don't overload your stove with wood. Learn how to make the stove adjustments so that you don't accidentally overheat the system.

Keep a freshly charged ABC dry chemical fire extinguisher near the stove. Again, think ahead and don't put it where a fire could keep you from reaching it, such as behind the stove. Don't laugh, I have seen many extinguishers stored there.

Don't use your stove for burning corrugated boxes, paper scraps, plastic, and wood from items such as power poles or crossties. If you use resin-rich pine for kindling, be sure to use just a little. I once had a cabin guest who used my pine kindling for wood in my stove, and if I hadn't returned to the cabin when I did, the cabin would have burned down. The stove and stovepipe were red hot. Make sure everyone knows how to operate the stove and the rules as to what to burn.

Have your chimney inspected once a year. In the backcountry, a member of the nearest volunteer fire department will probably do it for a small donation to his department. If the chimney needs cleaning, have someone do it who is experienced. I have seen some good chimney systems damaged by inexperienced chimney cleaners.

For taking out ashes, have a fireproof, airtight container to put them in for several days before spreading. I have seen hot coals smolder for days. Fresh ashes taken from a stove and spread in grass or leaves can lead to a grass or forest fire, and burn your cabin in the process.

Keep flammable materials away from the stove and never, never use flammable material such as kerosene, charcoal lighter fuel, or lantern fuel to start a fire.

Never throw an ice-covered log from the woodpile into a wood-burning stove. The severe temperature change can damage cast-iron stoves, and there is the danger of a vapor explosion. It is recommended that you keep the next day's wood supply on the cabin porch, covered up to keep it free from ice and snow.

Make sure everyone who uses your cabin knows the signs of a chimney fire: air sucking sounds, a loud roar, and shaking stovepipes. If this occurs, get everyone out and away from the cabin. Have someone call the fire department if one is near. Cut off the stove's air supply by closing the dampers. Open the stove and quickly spray the contents of your fire extinguisher into the stove's firebox. I am told this dry chemical is sucked up the chimney to the source of the fire. Be careful not to blow hot coals out of the stove. With the use of a good stove, a good chimney system, good wood, and regular chimney cleaning you should never have to experience the terror of a chimney fire.

## Wood Wisdom

Whether you heat your cabin with a fireplace or a wood-burning stove, you will need a supply of firewood. Also if you have an outside fire ring or cook in a bean hole you will need firewood for those as well.

At our cabin, early spring is when we start cutting and splitting firewood for the coming winter. It is looked upon as a fun family activity, and the results are a woodshed full of seasoned wood and a warm cabin for the next winter.

Before using a chain saw to cut firewood or for any cabin building or land management task, study the chain saw safety information in appendix 2.

Many claims have been made about the heating value of wood. It is difficult to give a precise answer on a wood's heating value because of these variables: (1) moisture content, (2) density, and (3) type of wood. A green or freshly cut tree may contain as much water as burnable material. If you burn green wood, a lot of energy is wasted in boiling off water, and it is dangerous due to creosote buildup in chimneys. Dried wood is easier to burn and more of the heat produced is transferred into the cabin instead of passing up the chimney as steam. If wood is moist and resinous, for example, fresh cut pine smoking may occur, which can ruin household belongings and form creosote in your chimney or flue. It is recommended that all firewood be thoroughly air dried before use as fuel.

The type of wood, hardwood or softwood, used for fuel affects its economy. See the firewood rating chart, appendix 3. While the heat value in terms of BTUs per pound does not vary greatly between hardwood and softwood, the density does. Less dense softwoods do not give as much energy per volume as hardwoods such as oak and hickory. In addition, the density of a wood is important since wood is usually bought by volume. The most common unit is the "cord," that is a stack of wood 4 feet wide, 4 feet high and 8 feet long. Sometimes wood is sold by the truckload, which is a highly variable measure. A rule of thumb is that a half-ton pickup truck is capable of carrying ⅓ cord of wood. To find out what fraction of a cord you are buying, use this formula: height of wood X width of wood X depth of wood divided by 128. The answer is the fraction of a cord.

The tighter the wood is packed, the more wood for your money. The denser the wood, the fewer trips you will have to make to the woodshed next winter. The relative merits among some firewood are illustrated in the table in this chapter.

## SOURCES OF FIREWOOD

With a little effort on your part and a one-time investment in tools, including chain saw, wedges, bow saw, ax, files, hearing protection, safety glasses, and maul, you can get wood for free or for little cost. If your cabin is sitting on wooded acreage, a rule of thumb is that with proper management, one cord of wood can be cut annually for each acre you own. (A local forest ranger or forester can advise you as to how to manage this forest.) This practice will keep your wood supply renewable as well as beautify your woodlands by removing old and diseased trees. Whether you cut in your wood lot or that of another, practice to prevent forest fires.

The U.S. Forest Service and some state forests have programs to permit the public to cut firewood of down or dead trees for little or no cost. Other free or low-cost sources of wood are utility company pruning, pulp and paper companies, sawmills, town dumps, and farmers clearing new ground. Always be sure to secure permission from the proper authorities.

As a side note, I always watch for new house construction when driving around. This is usually a good free source of pine building scraps, which can be split up into kindling. Most builders will be glad for you to haul it away. While this dry pine is not for firewood, it is great kindling.

You can usually find a local firewood dealer. When buying wood, be sure it is split and dry (why pay for water?), dense, and tightly packed. If you must buy green wood, buy it in the early spring since it takes months to dry (see next section). Be sure to measure the fireplace or stove, and have your firewood cut small enough to fit.

Cutting your own firewood is good exercise and can be a fun family outing; however, be sure to work safely, use the proper tools, and keep children away from the work area.

## SPLITTING, STACKING, AND SEASONING

Once you have the wood, how do you prepare it for burning? If it is moist, it should be air-dried before use. If the wood's diameter is greater than 8 inches, it should be split and the length cut small enough to fit your fireplace or stove and to stack easily in the woodshed. Split wood dries faster

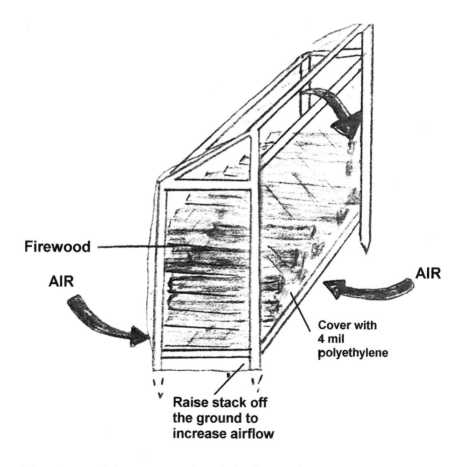

**Firewood**

**AIR**

**AIR**

**Cover with 4 mil polyethylene**

**Raise stack off the ground to increase airflow**

The solar wood dryer can speed up drying firewood.          Illustration by Blee than wood that is not split and is easier to stack. Stacking firewood off the ground will permit air to circulate freely in the woodshed and will help prevent ground rot.

Stacking the wood in a sunny location and covering it with clear plastic sheeting can accelerate the drying of wood. It is best to keep the plastic away from the ends of the woodpile to allow good airflow, which speeds the evaporation process.

An interesting and fast method for drying firewood is the use of a solar wood dryer. This easy to build device is simply a rack for stacking cut firewood off the ground. The rack is placed in a sunny spot near the cabin and loaded with wood. Next, the wood and rack are wrapped in clear plastic except the ends. A vent opening is designed into the top of the dryer. The sun and air speed up the drying process. This is a good method to dry wood if you are late in the season cutting your firewood. An illustration of this simple device is shown in this chapter.

One way to tell if wood is ready for burning is to weigh a few identified pieces on a bathroom scale. Record the weight and place the identified wood back into the woodpile. Wait a month, and then weigh the wood again. If the wood has lost weight, it is drying.

The author's woodshed also doubles as a house for an electric generator.

Photo by JWF

Another method for determining if wood is ready for burning is to examine the ends of the logs to see if cracks are appearing. Cracks appear only when wood is relatively dry.

Store your winter's supply of firewood in a woodshed to keep it dry and from getting scattered. My woodshed is small but it holds enough wood to keep my cabin warm for a winter of weekends. It is made from log siding to match the cabin and outhouse. A small room is enclosed in one end to house the generator and some yard tools. This room has a lockable door. The rest of the metal-roofed shed is for firewood. Overall, the shed measures 8 feet wide by 4 feet deep by 6 feet, 6 inches in the rear. In the front of the shed is a large wooden box that holds split kindling. I built the shed in one day, without help, so a woodshed is not a major project. In colder climates or where a cabin will be used more than for weekends, a larger shed would be necessary.

# Lighting Options For the Remote Cabin

The cabin lighting is taken for granted if you have electrical service. However, for the cabin that is self-sufficient, some planning is necessary in order to have light at night and run small appliances.

As I examined the options to achieve this, I looked at solar systems and wind turbine systems. There is a lot of merit to these systems, especially for cabin dwellers in a remote areas. They are more expensive to put in, however, and require technical knowledge and operational skills too involved to discuss in this book. Books and equipment to install systems are available from Lehman's. (See appendix 1.) The systems I cover in these pages are those most often used today in remote cabins.

## GAS/DIESEL GENERATOR

If you insist on having electric lights, perhaps a well with an electric pump, and the ability to run a few small appliances, then you will want to consider a generator. The decision to use a generator should be made before you build your cabin, as you will want to wire the cabin for lights, receptacles, pump, etc. as you build the structure.

When building my Cross Creek Hollow cabin, I wired it with two receptacles to make it possible to use electric lights. From the cabin, I ran an underground wire to my woodshed in which there is a small room for the generator. I have a Coleman Powermate Pulse 1750, which does a good job. In all honesty, I have only used the generator a few times. I prefer using propane lanterns to light the cabin. The radio is battery operated. I don't run any electrical appliances.

The gas/diesel fuel generator can supply electrical power to the most remote cabin. However, the wattage requirements for the cabin must match the capabilities of the generator.                                           Photo     by JWF

To choose a generator your first step should be to figure the total number of watts, including starting or surge watts, you will need a generator to supply. You will want a generator that has a greater wattage capacity than your needs, as generators that run at capacity or are overloaded will have a short life. The accompanying chart will give you wattage requirements for the various items that may be used in a remote cabin. The total wattage, including starting watts, will dictate the size generator you will need to buy. As an example, a generator with a maximum output of 5,000 watts can power six electrical circuits; enough to simultaneously operate several lights, a refrigerator, a radio, and a water pump.

There is a good selection of generators available. The size and features you want on a generator will determine what the unit will cost. Generators that run quietly or have remote starting cost more, but these features are nice to have. The run time of a generator is important to know. A generator with only three hours run time keeps you running outside to refuel the tank. A run time of six to eight hours will get you through a long evening without wading through the snow, in the dark, to refuel. You can refuel the following day in good light.

## AVERAGE WATTAGE REQUIREMENT GUIDE

| Cabin Use | Running Wattage Requirements | Additional Wattage Required for Starting |
|---|---|---|
| Coffee maker | 1,750 | 0 |
| Dishwasher—cool dry | 700 | 1,400 |
| Electric frypan | 1,300 | 0 |
| Electric range, 8" element | 2,100 | 0 |
| Microwave oven, 625 watts | 625 | 800 |
| Refrigerator or freezer | 700 | 2,200 |
| Automatic washer | 1,150 | 2,300 |
| Clothes dryer—electric | 5,750 | 1,800 |
| Lights | as indicated on bulb | 0 |
| Radio | 50 to 200 | 0 |
| Television—color | 300 | 0 |
| Central air conditioner | | |
| 10,00 BTU | 1,500 | 2,200 |
| **Portable Heater (kerosene, diesel fuel)** | | |
| 50,000 BTU | 400 | 600 |
| 90,000 BTU | 500 | 725 |
| 150,000 BTU | 625 | 1,000 |
| **Computers** | | |
| Desktop | 600 to 800 | 0 |
| Laptop | 200 to 250 | 0 |
| Monitor | 200 to 250 | 0 |
| Fax | 600 to 800 | 0 |
| Printer | 400 to 600 | 0 |

Average wattage requirement guide.

Other features you will want to consider in a generator will be a low-oil indicator and shutdown. Low oil will kill your generator quicker than anything. In addition, since you are in the woods a spark-arrest muffler is good to have, as is electronic ignition, automatic voltage regulator, and circuit breakers. If you want to keep your cabin temperature from dropping below freezing, there are automatic electric-start generators that have thermostat controls; this protects water pipes, etc. when you aren't at the cabin. Generators that produce both direct and alternating current can be used to charge deep-cycle batteries for DC appliances when the generator is off, further increasing their efficiency. Visit the web sites of companies such as Coleman Powermate, Craftsman, and Honda to compare generators and to obtain help in deciding which generator is best for your cabin.

Whether you or a professional electrician wires your cabin for a generator, you will want to make sure that the load center (electrical panel) is one that is made for generators. These make it easy to hook up or disconnect your generator and some generator load centers are designed to help you run your generator with an even load so the unit will last a lot longer. Gen/Tran Corp. is a company that specializes in load centers, and a visit to their web site will help you choose the load center that is right for your generator and cabin.

## CENTRAL LP (PROPANE) GAS SYSTEM

Anyone who has spent time in a recreational vehicle knows the convenience of a central LP gas system. It gives the users lights and fuel for the cook stove. In some cases, the refrigerator is run with gas. The same system can be installed in a cabin. It should be planned from the beginning and installed during the construction of the cabin by a certified gas-installation professional. Your local LP company can help you find the help you need.

The system usually consists of a fuel tank, a pressure regulator, and copper tubing running to all lights and appliances. The size fuel tank you will have will depend upon where your cabin is located. If it is in the service area of an LP company and has good access to a public road, then you may want to get a large tank that will only require filling every few months. If your cabin is really remote and difficult to reach, you may want to run the gas system with two small LP tanks and bring fuel with you each time you go to the cabin.

LP lighting fixtures require you to use a match or lighter to light the mantle in each light, and most of the ones I've seen project about as much light as a 65- to 70-watt electric light bulb. You can get wall-mounted or ceiling-mounted fixtures.

Cooking stoves designed for the LP system come in a variety of sizes. The two most popular sizes for remote self-sufficient cabins are the 20-inch and 30-inch four-burner models, which have an oven. Some models come with "instant on" burners, which do not require a match or lighter to start. Friends who cook with these stoves tell me they will do anything your home stove will do. At today's prices, the 20-inch model will cost you $369, and the 30-inch model will run about $389.

Gas refrigerators have been around for decades and are used very successfully in some of the most remote parts of the world. One of the best-known gas refrigerators is the Servel, made by a Swedish company and sold in Europe as Electrolux.

The simple LP refrigeration system works on the principle that heat makes cold through the natural cooling power of evaporation. A tiny flame heats an ammonia mixture permanently sealed inside the service-free cooling unit, generating a never-ending cycle of evaporation and condensation. The flame is thermostatically adjusted to maintain cooling. There are no moving parts, the refrigerators are quiet, and they are well made. I am told some of these refrigerators have been in use for over 50 years. They are available in sizes ranging from 1.9 cubic feet of interior space to 10 cubic feet. At this writing, the cost ranges from $539 to $1,500. For more information on all these LP products and LP systems, contact Lehman's.

## Propane Lantern Light

A bright, long-lasting, relatively safe light source for self-sufficient cabins is the propane lantern. I have used them for several years in my cabin, and not only are they bright and economical to burn, but everyone who stays at the cabin says they add something to the backwoods personality of the cabin.

I use Coleman's two-mantle propane lantern with electronic ignition. I have two lanterns in the living room of the cabin and one in the bedroom. I use a fourth lantern for cooking outside or for doing chores on the porch. These double-mantle lanterns, when turned up high, are about as bright as a 100-watt electric light bulb. The propane fuel source for the lantern is a 16.4-ounce propane cylinder. On a full cylinder, a double-mantle lantern will burn about 7 hours on high and 14 hours on low.

The electronic ignition is a great feature, as you don't need matches to light the lantern. Each lantern comes with a plastic base that makes it easy to place the lantern on a table or other level surface. For safety's sake, to give good lighting to the room and to protect the lantern from being accidentally knocked over or hit, I have a small chain hanging from an eye-hook in the ridgepole in the top of the cabin ceiling down to 7 feet above the floor, with

A traditional kerosene lantern requires a flame to start and is not typically as safe as the electric-ignition propane lantern (opposite page), which gives the cabin a bright, long-lasting light source.                    Photo by the Coleman Company

an S-hook in the last link of the chain. The lantern bail hooks in the S-hook. This system works well, although it takes a tall person to light the lantern.

Mantles need to be changed on these lanterns periodically, so I keep a supply of clip-on mantles on hand, and it takes little time to change them. In addition, I wash the globes on my lanterns often. A dirty globe gives poor lighting, and the few minutes it takes to wash the globe rewards my cabin with a bright light.

The author prefers to hang his cabin lighting from a chain from the ceiling for safety's sake.

Photo by JWF

There are several downsides to propane lanterns. The first complaint I usually hear is they make a hissing sound. To some this is a sound associated with camp life, to others an annoying noise. The lanterns can get very hot, and caution is necessary when handling them, or hands and fingers can get burned. Be sure not to hang them too close to combustible material, as a fire can result. I once hung a double-mantle lantern, by its bail, from a gun rack over a cabin door and sat down to read. Soon I smelled scorching wood. The top of the door facing was just short of bursting into flames when I realized what I had done.

As with all gas-fueled products, you must be cautious that propane lanterns, stoves, and other appliances are not leaking. Propane contains a fragrance, added by the fuel company, that has a distinct odor; and the first whiff of that odor should put you into action. A common mistake is to let a lantern run out of fuel. If the person replacing the cylinder doesn't turn the lantern off to put on a new cylinder, the gas will leak out into the unlit lamp. A tightly built cabin is a bomb when it is filled with propane gas. Learn how to handle propane and propane appliances safely, and instruct everyone who stays at your cabin in proper propane use.

## LIQUID-FUEL LIGHTING

Before Colonel E. L. Drake drilled the first oil well in Pennsylvania in 1859, lighting in America was basically candlelight. It was an inferior means of lighting that burned down many houses, barns, and businesses. In addition, it was a poor light to read or do chores by. With the discovery of oil came kerosene lamps and a whole new way of lighting.

Today gas or kerosene lamps and lanterns light many remote cabins and a few homes. Many of these lighting devices give out good light. The Coleman two-mantle Powerhouse propane gas lantern burns about as bright as a 100-watt electric bulb.

With a fuel capacity of two pints, it will operate 7 hours on high and 14 hours on low. Coleman also offers single-mantle gas lanterns, lanterns that will operate on either gas or kerosene, and a line of kerosene-only lanterns. These lanterns operate under pressure and require occasional pumping to give a bright light. They require periodic fillings with flammable liquid fuel, which means going out of the cabin to refuel. As liquid-fuel lanterns go, they are much safer than most such lamps and lanterns because the fuel is in a spill-proof tank, thus if accidentally knocked over, a fire is less likely.

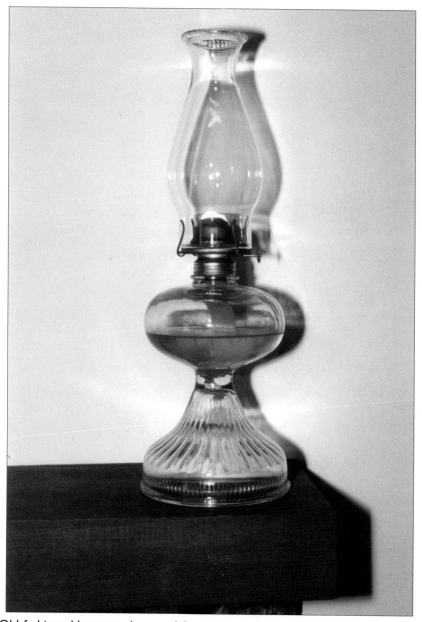

Old-fashioned kerosene lamps, while romantic, give low light and are a fire hazard if broken.

Photo by JWF

The Aladdin kerosene lamp will give a bright light for up to 40 hours on a gallon of kerosene.

Some people think a self-sufficient cabin is not complete unless the lights are the old-fashioned wick lamps. I have used these lamps in my cabins and they are better than candles, but they are no match for the propane gaslights. Perhaps my major concern with these traditional kerosene lamps is the potential for a serious fire if they get knocked over when lit. You have a fuel supply in a container that is not necessarily spill-proof. Sitting on top of that fuel supply is a flame. Put the two together in a broken or spilled lamp, and you have a cabin fire.

If you really want the economy and romance of a kerosene lamp, then consider the Aladdin lamp. The Aladdin lamp has been around since the early 1900s and produces light with an incandescent mantle that glows with a brilliant white light, light enough to read by. They require a warm-up period before you get the bright light. As for economy, these lights will operate for about 40 hours on a gallon of kerosene. For those who want a quality kerosene lamp and are willing to learn to use it correctly and safely, they make a good light. An Aladdin lamp at this writing will cost you from $90 to $200, depending on the model you like. A good source is the Lehman's or Cumberland General Store's catalog (see appendix).

## BATTERY LIGHTING

Lighting the cabin primarily with battery-powered lamps is not a good option. However, as a secondary source of light there is a place for battery lights. Instant light in the bedroom or bunk area can be supplied by a Coleman table lamp, which can operate for up to 17 hours with four D-cell alkaline batteries. This lamp uses a xenon bulb and has a shatter-resistant shade.

Any of a variety of battery-operated fluorescent lamps and lanterns offered by Coleman and American Camper will make a late-night trip to the outhouse or woodshed much easier. Often these lanterns are more convenient than a flashlight, as they have a handle that makes hanging them up much easier. I keep several near the bunks in my cabin.

It goes without saying to keep a good supply of batteries on hand and a spare bulb or two. They seem to need replacing just when you need the light.

With the rapidly changing technology in lighting that's going on today, especially in flashlights, I am sure we will soon be seeing the appearance of many more unique tools for lighting our way in the dark.

CHAPTER

# Sleeping
# Accommodations

O ver and over, people tell me the reason they built their cabin was for peace and quiet, the chance to catch up on some much-needed rest. Then you spend the night there, and after sleeping on their beds you wonder why they ever come to the cabin.

Usually the beds are cheap leftover twin beds the kids outgrew, complete with urine odor and lumpy mattresses. It makes you wonder why the kids didn't run away with the circus.

If not the kids' old beds, perhaps they are cheap bunk beds purchased from that discount furniture store that is always going out of business, you know, the ones you see in commercials on late-night TV. These are just as bad as the kid's beds mainly because today's bunk beds are designed for kids, short in length, with thin mattresses and the top bed just a couple of feet over the lower bed. Built for kid-size occupants, they shake like they are going to fall apart when an adult turns over. It's downright frightening to be on the lower bunk when your 250-pound fishing partner gets up during the night. Putting your boots on in the morning will almost guarantee a concussion from banging your head on the top bed rail.

There is nothing more fun than cabin life, but when you aren't getting the proper sleep you start thinking about selling the cabin and going to a resort on long weekends.

I have spent a sizable portion of my outdoor career not getting enough sleep. I have probably spent as many nights in a sleeping bag as under sheets. I don't mind sleeping bags; in fact, I really like good ones. It's the bunks and mattresses I have had to spend the night on that have caused my sleep deprivation. I have slept on canvas folding cots, military surplus bunk beds, built-in plywood beds, full-size beds that I am sure the homeless shelter threw out, and countless types of air and foam mattresses on thrown-together homemade bunk beds in camps and cabins across North America. I guess I thought that was just part of my career.

Then on a trip a few years ago I spent some time in Twin Oaks Hunting Lodge in south Texas and once again found myself on the top bed of a set of bunk beds. There was a pleasant difference this time; these bunk beds were made for full-grown men and designed to be comfortable. I couldn't believe it. They were sturdy, the ladder was made for heavy barefooted men with bad knees, the mattresses were quality-made adult-size twin mattresses, and the space between the bottom and top beds was enough to almost give you a nose-bleed if you slept on the top. A 6-foot man could sit on the bottom bed and put on his boots in complete comfort and safety. Each morning my hosts had trouble getting me to wake up, it was wonderful. I made myself a promise on that trip that I was going to build bunk beds like these for my cabin.

Not long after that, I mentioned the bunk beds to a friend. He informed me he had a set of plans for such a bunk bed that he had modified from a plan he saw in a magazine article. He boasted that the resulting bunk beds were perfect for large men and those smaller really enjoyed the space. I

You can build heavy-duty bunk beds that are tailored for adults.

got a copy of his plans and had a carpenter friend of mine make two sets of the bunks.

My friend built the bunks in his shop, but due to their size he had to assemble them in the cabin bedroom. They are put together so that if I ever want to move them, they can be easily disassembled. A plan for these bunk beds accompanies this chapter. The bedposts are made from 4-by-4-inch square post, and the side and foot/head boards are 2-by-2-inch boards. The side boards and foot/head boards are notched into the bedpost for added strength. The bed bottoms are made from ½-inch plywood which slides into a ½-inch routed groove into the side boards. All joints are glued and screwed. The 18-inch-wide ladder is made from 2-by-4-inch risers (sides) and rungs cut from 1½-inch closet poles. The ladder is notched to fit the top bunk's side board at a comfortable and safe angle. It can rest against the side of the top bunk or at the foot, depending on the space in the room. We sanded the bunks to prevent splinters and sharp edges, and left them unfinished to match the walls of the cabin.

My carpenter friend charged me $400 for materials and labor to build the beds. It turned out to be a good investment. Once the bunks were in place I purchased four adult twin-size quality mattresses to go on the beds. I have used them with extra-large sleeping bags and with sheets and blankets, and either way, considering you have your favorite pillow, they sleep as good

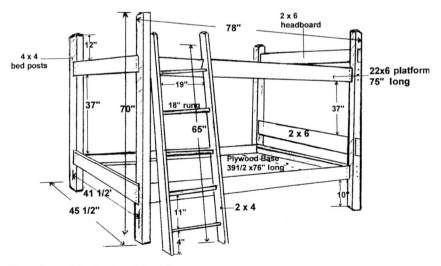

Plans for adult-size bunk-bed frames.                    Illustration by Blee

as the bed at home. No longer do we miss out on sleep at our cabin due to less-than-perfect beds.

The bunks have enough floor clearance to allow for several wide plastic storage boxes with lids. We use those to store clothing and other items used when staying at the cabin. A shelf has since been built above the head of each bed as a simple nightstand for items such as alarm clock, watch, wallets, change, and other items. A battery-operated, soft-glow night light is on each shelf to make midnight trips easier on everyone.

I have since added a 1-inch-by-6-foot guard rail on the outside edge of each top bunk, as a result of a mighnight mishap: One night the alarm clock, accidentally set, went off in the middle of the night and I sailed off the bunk, in the dark, to stop that obnoxious noise. I forgot how high the top bunk was, and I hit the floor much harder than I wanted. The cabin shook. Everyone in the cabin enjoyed the antics, but it was a wake-up call for me, as my grandchildren love to sleep on top. A child rolling off during the night could be very dangerous.

Regardless of whether you use these bunk beds or other beds of your choice, I highly recommend spending the money to have top-quality sleeping accommodations at your cabin. Good beds, mattresses, pillows, and bedding are just as important in a cabin as they are at home. The great outdoors is even greater when you get a good night's sleep and wake up each morning refreshed.

# The Outside Fire Ring— A Must for Any Cabin

The heart of the cabin is usually around the fireplace or stove. It is here that stories are told, friendships built, problems solved, adventures relived, and jokes told. There is something about fire; it keeps us warm, it permits us to cook our food, it entertains us, it keeps us company, and it relaxes us. However, the heart of the cabin, during mild weather, will move outside if you have a fire ring near your cabin. Here you get all of the above-mentioned benefits of fire plus lots of fresh air, a look at the heavens, more space, and if you wish, cooking facilities, all at the same time.

When I first built my cabin the fire ring was one of the first additions. I sited it 30 feet to the side of the cabin, aligned with the kitchen window so that we could see the fire ring and talk to anyone out there while we are cooking both inside and on the fire ring. My fire ring is a commercial-grade ring made from heavy steel, 30 inches across and 10 inches deep. It has a heavy-duty cooking grate hinged to one side, and when the grate is down on the ring it covers about 50 percent of the fire ring.

The fire ring was designed to sit on top of the ground; however, I dug an open hole and set the ring in the ground, permanently. Around the top I placed flat rocks in cement, making sure several of them were level so that I could cook with Dutch ovens and reflector ovens. The rocks also serve to keep the hot fire from catching the surrounding grass on fire. Since the fire ring is in the ground, I must shovel out ashes several times a year. This is a small price to pay for having the fire ring down out of the way.

I thought it would be difficult getting a fire going with the fire in a hole, but as of several hundred campfires later, it hasn't been a problem. I also have a chuck wagon–style cooking bar that goes across the fire ring. From

The heart of the cabin moves outside around the fire ring during days of mild weather.                                                                    Photo by JWF

Commercial fire rings make having an outside fire easy to manage with relative safety.                                                                    Photo by JWF

the steel bar hang S-hooks of different lengths that are used to suspend cast-iron cooking pots over the fire. The fire ring is the favorite gathering place for most visitors to the cabin, and a great place to cook. We'll talk more about setting up and using outdoor kitchens in chapter 16.

## COMMERCIAL FIRE RINGS

When I was looking for my fire ring I found it difficult to find a commercial source for them, and I was lucky to have a friend who had an extra one. Since then I have found several sources. A manufacturer with a good variety of fire rings is Pilot Rock Park Equipment Company. (See appendix 1.) They have fire rings with adjustable cooking grates. The grate tips back out of the way so as not to obstruct the view of people sitting around the campfire during storytelling sessions or sing-alongs. Here are some other features of these well-made fire rings:

- Flanged fire ring. The 1-inch top flange is both a safety feature and reinforces the ring against heat warpage.
- Infinite adjustment of cooking surface. You can adjust the grate for various cooking levels.
- Grate tips back for easy fire building. Grate will lift up and out of the ring for fire building and clean-out.
- Three fire barrier heights. Rings are available with 7-inch, 9-inch, or 11¼-inch height. Choose the degree of fire barrier you need.
- Unique handle design. The handle design allows the cooking grate to lower down inside the ring and keeps the spring grips out of the heat.
- Public-use-type spring grips. The spring grips are coiled from ½-inch steel flat-bar for a safer, cooler handle.
- Fire ring tips back for easy cleaning. The entire ring lifts up on hinges to make clean-out easy.
- Installs without a concrete pad. The fire ring may be installed on the ground or on gravel, avoiding the trouble and expense of a concrete pad.
- Conserves firewood. The cooking grate will lower down inside the ring, allowing the user to cook over a low fire.
- Reinforced grate foils vandalism. The structurally reinforced grate design is strong enough to deter vandalism.

Pilot Rock makes fire rings in a variety of diameters ranging from a wood-conserving 28 inches to a group size of 60 inches. Also they make models that are wheelchair accessible and models that are raised high enough for cooking comfort.

Where were these fire rings when I was looking for mine? If you don't like all the advantages of a commercial fire ring, you can make one from a large truck or tractor tire rim by taking a cutting torch and cutting out the middle. However, since the fire ring is an item you will probably buy only once for your cabin, why not get the commercial model with all the conveniences?

## CUSTOM BENCHES FOR YOUR FIRE RING

Most people interested in wildlife management know that the "father of modern wildlife management" was a professor and philosopher by the name of Aldo Leopold. This brilliant man had a cabin retreat which he called "The Shack" on his 120-acre farm in Wisconsin. He, like most of us with cabins, had a fire ring, and he designed a bench specifically for use around one.

South Carolina wildlife biologist Joe Hamilton studied the Leopold bench and saw its merits. He drew plans and has written articles on how the bench is made. It was from Joe that I learned how to make the benches. I now have three around my fire ring made by my son, Chris. They are most comfortable, and everybody who sees them wants one. The bench is designed so that the seat is very comfortable. It alleviates the pressure on one's bottom even though it is made from wood. When you first look at them, they look as though they lean too far to the rear, but Leopold knew what he was doing, as it is just the right angle to get very relaxed.

Here is how you can build your own for $30 or so.

I guess you could use almost any finished lumber, but Chris used pressure-treated Southern pine to build mine. Joe once sent me a photograph of a bench made from Eastern red cedar, and it was beautiful, too pretty to be sitting outside around a fire ring.

The bill of material is short:

Two boards 2 by 8 by 24 inches, for the rear legs.
Two  boards 2 by 8 by 42 inches, for the front legs.
One board 2 by 10 by 46 inches, for the bench seat board.

The Leopold bench is a sturdy, easy-to-build bench design for use around the campfire.

Photo by JWF

One board 2 by 10 by 49 inches for the backrest, it must reach the outside edges of the front legs.

Six ⁵⁄₁₆-inch carriage bolts 3 inches long, with nuts and washers.

Twelve 3-inch deck screws (to secure the backrest to the front leg supports and to secure the bench seat to the tops of the rear leg supports.)

Begin by cutting the ends of the front legs at a 55-degree angle, with an overall length of 36 inches. Cut the ends of the rear legs at a 55-degree angle, with an overall length of 16½-inches.

Next, the backrest should be cut to 49 inches, to reach outside of the tops of the front legs. Adjust a skill-saw at a 35-degree angle, and cut the top edge of the backrest; this will allow the backrest to fit flush with the tops of the front legs. Cut a notch for the backrest to fit into the back side of the top portion of each front leg. Cut the bench seat to 46 inches.

Now you are ready to assemble the bench. Draw a line at a 55-degree angle on the inside of each front leg 16½-inches from the bottom of the leg. Align the rear leg with the pencil mark on the front leg, secure with a C-clamp; and drill three ⁵⁄₁₆-inch holes through both legs. Countersink the holes on the inside of the legs to allow for a washer and a nut. Insert the car-

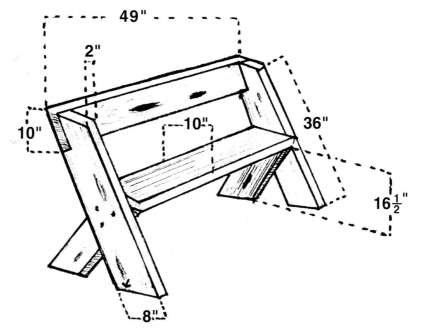

Building for the Leopold bench.

Illustration by Blee

riage bolts from the outside, place a washer and a nut on each bolt, and tighten. Drill three holes the diameter of the deck screws through the bench seat 1 inch from the ends. Position the bench seat and secure it to the top of each rear leg, using the 3-inch deck screws.

Finally, drill three holes in each end of the backrest. Attach the backrest to the cut-out sections of the tops of the front legs, using the 3-inch deck screws. Sand the boards. You now have your own Leopold bench.

I finished my benches by staining them to match the cabin and then put on a sealer. If you used pressure-treated wood you don't have to do anything to them.

There is nothing more fun than a cool evening around a fire in your commercial-grade fire ring, sitting on a Leopold bench and visiting with family or close friends.

If you do put in a fire ring at your cabin, be sure to put up another cord or so of firewood in your woodshed, as you will need it.

# Cabin Water Supply

A cabin with indoor plumbing and hooked to a public water system doesn't require much thinking on the part of the owner. However, if the cabin is remote, far from public utilities, one must give a lot of thought as to how the water needs for the cabin are going to be met. The choice is based on what is locally available and how much trouble and expense the cabin owner is willing to endure.

## Types of Wells

The first source of water many people think of when looking at a potential cabin site is a well. There are four types of wells, and you should know a little about each.

Dug wells are getting to be a thing of the past. They are dug by hand shovel to below the water table until incoming water exceeds the digger's bailing rate. The well is lined with stones, bricks, tile, or other material to prevent collapse, and is covered with a cap of wood, stone, or concrete. Water is usually drawn by hand.

Bored wells are large-diameter wells like those that are hand dug. They are bored by power equipment and are typically lined with concrete tile. Because of the type of construction, bored wells can go deeper beneath the water table than hand-dug wells.

Dug and bored wells have a larger diameter and expose a large area to the aquifer. These wells are able to obtain water from less-permeable materials such as very fine sand, silt, and clay. Some disadvantages of this type of well are that they are shallow and lack continuous casing, making them subject to contamination from nearby surface sources, and they go dry during periods of drought if the water table drops below the well bottom.

Driven wells are constructed by driving small-diameter pipe into shallow water-bearing sand or gravel. Usually a screened well point is attached to the bottom of the casing before driving. These wells are relatively simple and economical to construct, but they can tap only shallow water and, like dug wells, are easily contaminated from nearby surface sources.

Bored and driven wells, in remote locations where electricity is not available, usually have a hand pump installed to bring the water to the surface. Pumps of this type are relatively inexpensive, starting at about $150 and available from Cumberland General Store and Lehman's. (For these and other suppliers and manufacturers mentioned in this chaper, you'll find contact information in the appendix.)

Drilled wells are the most common wells today due to their record of usually producing a safe and continuous water supply. However, they can be expensive, depending on how deep they are drilled. Drilled wells are constructed by either percussion or rotary-drilling machines. Drilled wells that penetrate unconsolidated material require installation of casing and a screen to prevent inflow of sediment and collapse. They can be drilled more than 1,000 feet deep. To prevent contamination by water draining from the surface downward around the outside of the casing, the space around the casing must be sealed.

I had a well drilled on my farm just before I started working on this book, and we stopped drilling when the well was producing 15 gallons per minute. You want a well that has a flow of at least five gallons per minute for your cabin. We reached this flow at 220 feet. As with most drilled wells, the driller installed a submersible electric pump. The total cost for the well with pump was $2,500.

If you decide to have a well for your cabin, insist on a drilled well and select the driller after checking out his references carefully. Not all areas can produce well water of drinkable quality or at a reasonable depth, so check out the record of wells in the area around the cabin and do not hesitate to get the county health department involved in your decision, as they have lots of experience with wells in your region. Also keep in mind that many well drillers want their money regardless of whether they get you satisfactory water or not. Know all the details before you start drilling. Remember too that you will need a source of electrical power to run the pump. (See chapter 12.)

## SPRINGS

There are very few things nicer to have near the self-sufficient cabin than a clear bubbling spring; that is, if the water is safe to drink and the spring runs during drought just like it does during periods of high rainfall. There is a common belief that all spring water is safe to drink. Don't bet your life on it. Some springs are contaminated from natural sources and some from surface runoff. Before you decide to build your cabin near a spring, have your health department test the water and check out the recent history of the spring's flow, especially during periods of drought.

If the spring is higher in elevation than the cabin then you can build a holding tank at the spring and have water gravity-fed to the cabin. Where I grew up, lots of farmhouses had this type of water system.

## CREEKS, STREAMS, LAKES, AND RIVERS

Many cabins are built near lakes and flowing streams; however, gone are the days when you can get your drinking and cooking water from these sources and use it untreated. It is sad but true that in the most remote wilderness, as well as in populated areas, you cannot trust water from streams and lakes. Our need for safe drinking water has given rise to many myths about what is safe water. Many backwoodsmen have told me that water running swiftly over rocks and gravel gets purified. I know one fellow who swears that water is purified as it tumbles over the ninth rock. Don't believe any of these claims! Water running over rocks may be aerated, but not purified.

One of the dangers in wilderness lakes and streams, as well as waters in more populated areas, is giardiasis, caused by a one-celled parasite called *Giardia lamblia*. These small protozoans are a little larger than a red blood cell and inhabit the small intestine of their hosts, which are often beaver, cattle, dogs, and other animals, including man. This tiny parasite is passed from the host animal in fecal material and finds its way into streams and lakes. The person drinking from these waters is in for a horrible illness. *Giardia* are found in streams from the Arctic south. We will talk more about water purity a little later.

At my cabin we use creek water that we purify by boiling, for washing dishes, bathing, and other domestic needs. We bring the water to the cabin in a bucket. The grandchildren love this chore. However if you don't want to carry water to your cabin you can install a holding tank, which you can buy in a variety of sizes at home improvement stores or farm supply stores, and pump the water to the tank. Two of the most popular types of pumps are the portable gasoline engine–driven water pump, and the amazing ram pump.

## WATER PUMPS

The easiest way to get water from a lake or stream to a storage tank at your cabin is to use a portable gasoline-driven water pump. There are lots of these little pumps on the market. A lightweight example is the Honda WX 15. It weighs only 20 pounds yet can pump 72 gallons per minute. If speed is what you are interested in, the Kawasaki KWN20A is a 55-pound water pump that can pump 158 gallons per minute. Think how long it would take you to fill a 500-gallon storage tank. Not long! When using these pumps it is critical that they be used with a strainer on the intake, as even the clearest lake or stream will have particles of debris that will get into the pump and water supply.

Another option is the efficient ram pump. There is nothing new about the ram pump as it has been around since the 1700s. It is not suitable for lakes, as it requires moving water to work, but is a great pump for moving water from a creek to a storage tank. This simple pump is quiet, requires little maintenance, needs no electricity, and has few moving parts. Setting it up is simple: Put the intake pipe in the stream so the stream is flowing into the intake. Place the standpipe and ram pump downstream where there is at least 2 feet of fall. From the pump, run the delivery pipe uphill (you can go several hundred feet) to the storage tank.

Depending upon the ram pump, you can get from 800 gallons to 6,000 gallons per day. A strainer is necessary for the intake pipe to keep debris out of the system. These pumps cost from $350 to $750 and last for years. They are available from Lehman's or Cumberland General Store.

Remember, water taken from lakes or streams for human consumption will need to be purified after it is pumped to the cabin. (See "Making Water Safe," below)

## HAUL IT IN

If you install a water storage tank at your cabin, you can always haul in treated city water or well water from home, if you live in a rural community, and dump it into the tank. Also you can use plastic five-gallon portable water carriers, such as those made by Coleman or Reliance. Bring several each time you use the cabin. For years I have brought five of these containers filled with water before I leave home. They are used for drinking or cooking water. For running water at the sink I keep a five-gallon insulated container of water, with an easy on/off spigot, on the edge of the sink for cooking use. Another such container is available on the cabin porch for drinking water.

Safe water may be brought to the cabin in five-gallon containers.

Photo by JWF

## MAKING WATER SAFE

If you get cabin water from a questionable site such as a lake, stream, shallow well, or spring, you will want to make it safe. As I stated earlier, you can get giardiasis almost anywhere. Also many forms of waterborne bacteria, viruses, and protozoa are found in unsafe water. The Center for Communi-

Water taken from most natural sources should be filtered before being consumed.                                        Photo by JWF

cable Diseases estimates that 1,000,000 people in the United States get sick from microbiologically contaminated water each year and 1,000 die as a result. In short, make the water you use in your cabin safe.

One of the best methods of treating water is the boiling method. Boiling water for ten minutes or longer will produce germ-free water for drinking or cooking. Since boiling leaves water with a flat taste, you should pour it back and forth between two containers several times once it has cooled. This aerates it, restoring its natural taste.

There are a number of water filtration units that can give you safe water for your cabin. Many of these units are compact but can produce safe water fast. As I was working on this book I had the chance to use a PUR Guide model while staying at a remote cabin in central Oregon. We pumped water from a small brook using the Guide and got a quart of safe water about every 36 strokes of the handle. It was amazing how fast this little water filter would produce safe water.

For several years I have used a Katadyn Pocket Filter for filtering my water when traveling and living in remote areas, worldwide. Like the PUR unit, this system uses micro-filtration of water to remove microorganisms. This compact system produces about a quart of water per minute. These units range in price from under $100 to $200. For a micro-filter system with a higher output, consider the Katadyn Expedition Filter, which will filter up to a gallon of safe water per minute. The Expedition sells for around $900.

## INCLUDING THE KITCHEN SINK

If you have running water, then you will most likely have a kitchen sink. However, many builders of self-sufficient cabins don't put in a sink. I think this is a mistake, for it is a lot of work to empty dishpans of water outside, especially during the winter, and not have a sink to use in preparing meals.

Even though I don't have running water in my cabin, I built a kitchen sink into the counter/cabinet in a central location in the kitchen. It drains through PVC pipe to an underground 55-gallon grease pit I filled with pea gravel. The lower half of the drum has lots of holes for the water to drain.

I keep a five-gallon container of water with a spigot, on the edge of the sink. The sink makes handling water in the cabin clean and easy. It works great for preparing meals, washing dishes, etc.

The author installed a sink in this cabin and uses a 5-gallon water container with spigot to provide running water for cooking.                    Photo by JWF

# Planning the Remote Cabin Kitchen

I f you want a cabin with a modern kitchen, complete with microwave oven, electric range, refrigerator, and other conveniences, then you won't find this chapter very exciting. However, if you are one of us who likes the independence of being self-sufficient in a remote cabin, here is the fun part of cabin living: cooking using camping and pioneer skills.

## KEEPING PERISHABLES COOL

The cabin refrigerator can vary, depending upon whether or not you have power. If you have electricity run to your cabin or a powerful generator, then you can have a large refrigerator. If you have a central LP gas system you can have one of the efficient gas refrigerators described in chapter 12. But what if you have neither?

My first choice is a simple system of two insulated coolers. One is a 150-quart-size Igloo cooler in which I store meats, milk, and other foodstuffs. This cooler (where we usually place two blocks of ice) stays closed except when we get food out to prepare a meal. The second cooler, a 58-quart Coleman Xtreme, contains drinks and any other items that might be needed frequently. One block of ice goes in here. This cooler is usually opened more often. Using this system will get me through about four days during the summer and six days during the winter before I have to make an ice run. Keeping the cooler out of the sun and the lid closed as much as possible for either cooler is the trick. Always use block ice when you can get it, as it will last days longer than crushed ice. If you want crushed ice for drinks, put a bag of it in the small cooler, but use block ice to keep the cooler cold.

Perishables can be stored for long periods of time in an ice chest using block ice.

Photo by JWF

There are other coolers available that will run off your car's cigarette lighter, but these aren't usually large enough for a long stay at the cabin.

## CABIN COOKING

The cabin that is cut off, utility-wise, from the rest of the world can be an interesting place to cook and eat dinner. Part of the meal—say bread—may be baking in a little metal oven sitting on the wood-burning stove, with coffee and carrots steaming on the two-burner camp stove sitting on the cabinet next to the sink, beans simmering in the bean hole out behind the cabin, a roast cooking in a Dutch oven in coals next to the fire ring; and a pie baking in the reflector oven on the opposite side of the fire ring.

Those who cook on the modern range and oven at their cabin have the best in conveniences, but they are missing out on the simple pleasures of camp cooking and the delicious meals that come with it.

At Cross Creek Hollow, the visitor will most likely see a meal being cooked as described above. If we are in a hurry and there are just a couple of us staying there, we may cook the meals on the two-burner propane camp stove. For a larger group we may put the three-burner propane stove on the porch and cook. From there we move to the outside. The fire ring and the bean hole are considered part of the kitchen.

## PROPANE CAMP STOVES

For the same reasons I mentioned in chapter 12 in the section on liquid-fuel lighting, I don't use liquid fuel in stoves in the cabin. For many years I have used the Coleman two-burner propane stove. When more or hotter burners are needed, I break out the stove stand and set the Coleman Guide Series three-burner propane stove on it. The smaller stove uses 16.4-ounce propane cylinders and the larger stove hooks up to a 20-pound bulk propane tank. The smaller stove has two burners that put out 10,000 BTUs and it has electronic ignition. The larger stove has two burners that burn at 10,000 BTUs and one that burns at 15,000 BTUs.

As a safety note, I would never bring the 20-gallon propane tank into the cabin. It is a far greater risk if a leak should develop.

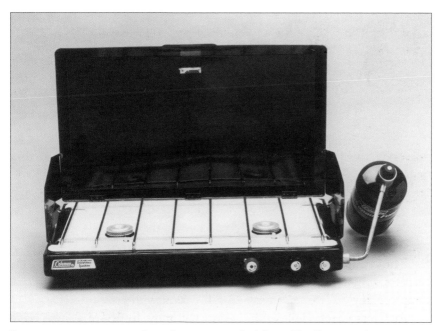

Propane camp stoves such as this one are ideal for self-sufficient cabins.

Photo by the Coleman Company

## CABIN CAMP STOVE OVENS

For baking in the cabin I use two unique camp ovens made by Fox Hill Corp. Each of these ovens will fit nicely on the wood-burning stove or on the propane camp stoves. They bake as well as any modern oven once you learn how to use them. The smaller one, called the Sportsman's Oven, is ideal for four or fewer people and has one rack. It is made from heavy-duty aluminum and measures 10 by 10 by 6 inches. The larger oven is called the Outfitter Oven and is similar to the other but has two racks and measures 10 by 10 by 9½ inches. They both have a temperature gauge in the front.

Coleman makes a camp oven from aluminized steel that has a front door with a temperature gauge in it. The rack in the oven is adjustable, and the oven will fold flat for carrying.

## COOKING ON THE WOOD STOVE

Many wood-burning stoves have a flat surface designed for cooking and do a good job of holding an even heat. However, I have found that propane camp

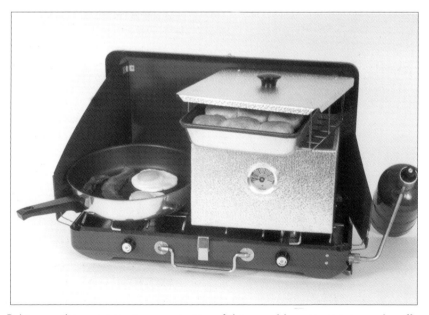

Baking on the propane stove or on top of the wood-burning stove may be efficiently done with the Fox Hill oven.                    Photo by the Fox Hill Corporation

stoves do a better job, and I only use my wood-burning stove for baking with one of the above-mentioned ovens. It is easy to burn yourself on a cast-iron stove if you accidentally touch it. The stove can be a job to clean if food spills on it, and it is hot to stand next to while cooking. My advice is to use your wood-burning stove for heating and use other means for preparing meals.

## FIREPLACE COOKING

Many cabin owners who have fireplaces want to cook in them, as did our forefathers. Granted, the fireplace can produce a great meal when a Dutch oven or reflector oven is used, but as with the wood-burning stove I think it is best to cook somewhere else. Spilled food on the hearth is a mess to clean up, and the smallest amount remaining attracts insects and mice.

## MOVING OUTSIDE—THE DUTCH OVEN AND FIRE RING

When you move outside the cabin for cooking, there seems to be more fun in the meal preparation. Even those who have never spent time in the outdoors enjoy the outdoor kitchen and the age-old cooking techniques.

Cooking in one or more Dutch ovens next to the fire ring is an easy way to fix a tasty meal. You can read one of the books written on Dutch oven cooking to master the art, but here is a little information to get you started at your cabin fire ring.

The Dutch oven has been used since America's frontier was along the Atlantic seaboard. In those early days, most cooking was done outdoors, in a fireplace, or in a lean-to behind the cabin. The settlers made a large cast-iron pot, with a flat lid, that could be placed directly into the coals of an open fire. Heat was distributed evenly throughout the pot since it was constructed of heavy cast iron. Early cooks learned that by heaping hot coals onto the flat lid, this newly designed pot could be used for baking, and roasting was improved.

Today, the true Dutch oven can only be purchased in such places as hardware stores, Boy Scout supply dealers, and a few outdoor equipment mail-order houses; or they may be purchased from the manufacturer, Lodge Manufacturing Company. (See appendix 1.) When buying a Dutch oven, make sure you are getting the real thing. It is made of heavy cast iron, with a flat bottom, sitting on three short legs protruding about 2-inches. It will

Dutch oven cooking is an age-old technique that still can be enjoyed at the cabin.

Photo by JWF

have a strong wire bail. The lid is made of the same heavy cast iron and will have a small handle in the center. The rim of the lid is flanged so that hot coals will stay on the lid while cooking.

You can get Dutch ovens in several sizes, usually from 8-inches to 16-inches in diameter, and from 4-to-6 inches deep. The 12-inch-diameter size is the most popular for family-size cooking. The weight ranges from 7 to 30 pounds. One word of caution: many modern-day flat-bottomed pots are called Dutch ovens. Make sure you are getting the one described above, which is specifically designed for open-fire cooking.

## Preparing the Dutch Oven for Use

With a your new Dutch oven the first step is to make sure the lid will seat well on the pot. If it does not, smear valve-grinding compound on the rim and the edge of the lid, and then rotate the lid until you have a good, tight fit. After getting the lid to seat properly, give the Dutch oven a good cleaning with hot water and soap. Thoroughly scrub the pot with a stiff bristle brush. This should be the only time your Dutch oven will be washed with soap. This washing process is necessary because manufacturers coat new Dutch ovens with protective waxes or oils that must be washed off before the oven is used.

The next step is the most important one: breaking the oven in, often called "sweetening." Since all cast iron is porous, breaking it in is essential if the Dutch oven is to perform at its best. There are many ways to do this, but the one method used most often is to nearly fill the oven with good-quality cooking oil and have a fish fry, keeping the oil hot until it works out to the exterior of the pot. Be sure the underside of the lid gets the same oil treatment. Another method of sweetening the oven is to smear all the surfaces of the pot and lid with a heavy coat of cooking oil. Next, put them into your home oven with the temperature set on 350 degrees Fahrenheit. Bake the Dutch oven for an hour. This can be a smoky job. You will want to open a few windows and cut off the smoke alarm.

Once the sweetening process is completed the Dutch oven should never again be washed with soapy water. Surprisingly, the oven will usually wipe clean without any strong detergents or scrubbing. With reasonable care and use, the Dutch oven will last a lifetime and get "sweeter" each time it is used.

# Dutch Oven Cooking

Now properly sweetened, your Dutch oven is ready for use. The most versatile piece of cooking gear available, it can be used for deep-frying, shallow frying, roasting, baking, boiling, or stewing. You can cook with either dry heat or moist heat. With the Dutch oven you are limited only by your imagination.

For baking, I have found that a round cake rack placed in the bottom raises the pan up higher like an oven rack making it better for baking and browning top crust. It keeps food from sticking to the bottom and makes cleaning up easier.

If you are using more than one Dutch oven, try "stack cooking" to give you more room around the fire ring. After you have the first Dutch oven heating properly, set the second on top of the first and add hot coals to its lid. I have seen outfitters stack as many as five Dutch ovens and serve a camp full of hungry hunters quickly as a result. I have settled on using a 14-inch oven for my main course with a smaller 10-inch oven sitting on top of it baking bread at the same time.

It is possible to bake two dishes in the Dutch oven at once if they require about the same heat and same amount of cooking time. Simply place each foodstuff in a separate pan and place the pans in the oven on the cake rack.

The Dutch oven lid, when turned upside down and placed on a small bed of hot coals, makes an excellent frying pan.

In order to handle the hot ovens and to move hot coals, I carry three (and what I consider essential) tools with my Dutch ovens. The first is a short-handled army surplus shovel used for spreading coals, placing coals on the lid, and digging pits for cooking. The second tool is a short fireplace poker that I have bent into a hook at the bottom. This poker allows me to move a hot oven, to lift a hot lid when checking food, and to move charcoal briquettes around for proper spacing. The third tool is a whisk broom that I use to sweep ashes off the lid before looking inside the pot.

I store my Dutch ovens, stacked, behind the stove in my cabin. You can get many Dutch oven recipes by going to the International Dutch Oven Society web site.

## REFLECTOR-OVEN BAKING

This highly efficient oven, handed down from early pioneer days, has contributed much to wilderness camps throughout North America. It has also

The fire ring outside the cabin offers many possibilities for outdoor cooking.

Photo by JWF

been used in many cabins, in conjunction with a fireplace, wood-burning stove, or outside fire ring, to produce excellent meals. Tasty breads, pies, cakes, biscuits, puddings, roasted meat and fish, and casseroles can be cooked in this simple oven. Any foods that can be cooked in the home oven can be baked in the reflector oven at your cabin.

In order to learn how to use a reflector oven, you must first understand the principles by which it works. The reflector oven is made from polished aluminum or polished sheet metal. It is constructed so that dry heat from a nearby fire is reflected from the walls of the oven around the food. The secret of even cooking with the oven is to protect the shiny surfaces of the metal to create the most efficient heat reflection. These surfaces should be washed with soft wool pads and non-abrasive soap when they get dull from use. When not in use or when being transported, the oven should be carried in a soft cloth bag.

Most reflector ovens are constructed so that they can be folded into a neat package measuring a foot square by half an inch thick. Weighing a pound or more, they are not usually found in a backpacker's camp but are excellent for base camps, canoe camps, or for cabins.

A reflector oven can be made from aluminum foil. Simply take a roll of heavy-duty aluminum foil and tear off a 24-inch sheet. Fold it in half so that the shiny sides are together, then open the fold out to form a 45-degree angle. Wrap the foil around sticks to make the V-ridge. Next, close the ends on each side of the V-ridge with more aluminum foil. Turn the V-ridge on its side with the opening toward the fire. With a little practice and imagination you can make a very efficient reflector oven from aluminum foil.

The optimum fire for reflector-oven cooking is one that has some hot flames. The best results come from a fire that has a back-log or sheet of aluminum foil placed upright across the fire from the reflector oven. This reflects the heat into the oven, which should be only 12 inches from the flames. As with any type of open-fire cooking, experience will soon teach you how to regulate the heat in the oven by moving it closer to or farther from the fire. Building the fire up or letting it burn down can also adjust heat. Two reflector ovens can be best used when they are placed across the fire from each other so that they are facing each other. This way they can reflect heat into each other.

Diane Thomas, wilderness cooking expert and author of *Roughing It Easy,* states that it is possible to learn to guess the temperature in a reflector oven with reasonable accuracy by holding your hand just in front of the

Using a reflector oven is an efficient way to bake outdoors.          Photo by JWF

oven. If you can hold it there for only one or two seconds, the temperature is 500 degrees Fahrenheit. If you can hold it there for three to four seconds, it's 400 degrees, six seconds, it's 300 degrees, and seven to ten seconds, 200 degrees. When cooking with a reflector oven, keep an eye on the food to be sure it is cooking properly. Turn the food every few minutes to make sure it is cooking evenly.

One of the joys of reflector-oven cooking is that you do not have to be choosy about the wood you use on the fire. Since the food is not cooked over the flames, it will not be affected by the use of pine or other softwoods. When cooking with a reflector oven, you can enjoy watching the food bake while you sit around the campfire or around your cabin fireplace.

## BEAN HOLE COOKING

A favorite method of cooking in hunting and fishing camps in the northeastern United States and Canada is what is commonly called "bean hole cooking." Dating back to early colonial days, this method of baking in a hole in the ground has survived several hundred years of improvements in ovens and baking techniques. Back before electric and gas stoves were common, logging camp cooks, remote resort lodge cooks, hunting and fishing camp cooks, and homestead cooks did much of their baking in cast-iron Dutch ovens in a hole filled with hot coals and covered with dirt. Because beans were the most common dish baked, the term "bean hole cooking" became the name of this technique.

Each year I hunt and fish with Pam and Ken French from their log cabin camp, named Camp Quitchabitchin, in central Maine. Outside their cabin, down near the lakeshore, Ken has built a permanent bean hole. Miss Pam prepares her tasty dishes that require baking, and Ken places the covered cast-iron pot into the hot coals in the bean hole. The lid is placed on top of the hole and it is covered with dirt. After a day of hunting or fishing we return, uncover the pot or pots, and the evening meal is hot and ready to eat.

Following Ken's instruction I have built a permanent bean hole at my cabin in Cross Creek Hollow. Now it is the center of attention anytime I am cooking for a group of guests. Here is how you can build your own permanent bean hole.

Take a clean 55-gallon steel drum and cut it in half. Save the lid to use as a cover, and discard the upper half. In a safe area, outside your cabin or camp,

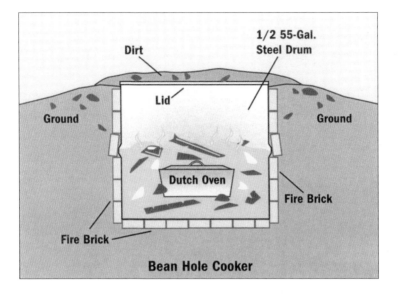

Plans for making a bean hole.                                    Diagram by JWF

dig a hole a little deeper and wider than the half drum. Line the bottom and side of the hole with fire bricks. Next drill several small holes in the bottom of the drum to allow water to drain in the event it should ever get inside. Place about 3 inches of sand in the bottom of the drum to prevent it from burning out. Put the drum in the fire brick–lined hole and fill in the spaces between the bricks, and between the bricks and drum, with sand. Place the lid on top of the drum, and you have a permanent bean hole.

When you want to bake a pot of beans or any other dish, simply build a fire in the bean hole. Leave the top off and let the hole get hot. Next, place a cast-iron Dutch oven filled with your favorite recipe for baked beans into the bed of coals in the bean hole, and put a couple of shovels full of hot coals on top of the Dutch oven. Put the cover on top of the drum, and cover it with dirt or sand. This will keep the temperature even for a long period of time. Go hiking or fishing for the day and return to a hot meal. As with most methods of cooking it will take a few trials to get the method perfected. Once it is worked out, it will become a favorite method of baking at your cabin.

## ORGANIZING THE KITCHEN

How well you organize your small cabin kitchen will determine how much room you will have for other activities and how easy it will be to find kitchen items when you need them. Since most cabins are solidly built with logs, log siding, or thick wood interiors, there are usually plenty of places to put hangers, on walls or exposed beams. Most small cabins have frying pans hanging from a wall or ceiling, adding character to the cabin.

In my cabin there is an exposed beam that runs overhead in the kitchen area, from which I hang eight skillets. The walls near the stove have nails at convenient locations to hang pots and pans. To the right of the sink next to a window there is an iron kitchen tool rack that I bought in a junk store. From it hang spoons, ladles, measuring cups, dippers and spatulas. Almost everyone who visits the cabin wants to buy the rack.

Under the sink cabinets is a good place to store kitchen cleaning supplies, dishpans, and paper goods. A tall stack of shelves can be built easily at home that will serve as a pantry for canned goods, spices, cooking oil and

In a small, self-sufficient cabin all available kitchen space is organized for cooking.
Photo by JWF

other staples. For storing fruit and fresh root vegetables, get a hanging wire vegetable basket. These are inexpensive and will hold a lot of vegetables.

Have a set of drawers or a secure box to keep knives and pointed kitchen tools away from children. It is amazing how many kitchen items you can have in the kitchen area of a small cabin, and yet they certainly are convenient when you need them. My kitchen area is the part of the cabin most often photographed by visitors.

Be sure to have comfortable places for people to sit when eating. Most small cabins have an eating table with four chairs around it. This serves as a game table or work table to do chores when not in use for meals. I have been in some cabins where a picnic table was used. Usually they were larger than necessary and it was easy to bang your knees up trying to walk around the benches. I have two large picnic tables at my cabin, but they are outside near the fire ring. We use them for cooking tables when we cook outside. On nice days we eat all our meals at the picnic tables. I have a lantern holder that clamps onto the tabletop so eating outside at night is pleasant.

One of the kitchen practices at my cabin is that all foods except canned goods go home when we go home. No perishable foods, no foods that mice or insects can get into, stay at the cabin other than when being used. Also, no liquids are left open when the cabin is vacant. If you eliminate the food and liquids that mice and insects seek and must have to survive, then you will not have these pests. There have been mice in my cabin twice in ten years, due to the cabin's tight construction; both times the door had been left open when no one was around. Both occasions the mice were found dead due to the lack of food and water. They got in and couldn't get out, and there was nothing in the cabin for their survival.

# Cabin Security

A t last, the weekend! You have worked hard all week. The one thing that has kept you going was the knowledge that the cabin was waiting for you and your family. Everyone looked forward to Friday night and going to the cabin.

Late Friday afternoon you and your family pack up the car and head to the woods. You pull into the cabin yard long after dark. The kids are awake now and talking about what they're planning to do this weekend. As you drive up to the cabin though, you get a sinking feeling as you see the front door standing open. You know what it is before you get the flashlight and walk up the steps—your cabin has been broken into. The week just got worse, and the weekend is ruined.

Seclusion is what your cabin in the woods is all about, but that same feature increases the possibility of your cabin being broken into or vandalized. While you are never completely free from the threat of burglary or vandalism, just as your home in town is never completely protected, you can do several things to protect your investment.

## SECURING YOUR PROPERTY

First have insurance on your cabin and its contents. Start shopping for insurance as soon as you make the decision to build a cabin. Talk to your insurance agent and see if you can add the cabin to your homeowner's policy. If not, get your agent to recommend a policy. I know of several cabin owners who had difficulty getting insurance in the cities where they lived, but local insurance agents who lived in the same county as the cabin

Building your cabin out of sight behind a locked gate will keep intruders to a minimum.

locations welcomed the business and were familiar with policies covering remote cabins.

Try to build your cabin where it is out of sight of roads. There is a lot of truth in the old saying, "out of sight, out of mind." The more visibile your cabin, the more tempting it is for lowlifes who ride around looking for trouble.

If possible, install a strong metal gate at the point where your camp road or driveway leaves the public road and keep it locked. If this is not possible, put up a gate partway down the driveway at the first suitable spot. The harder it is for someone to get a vehicle to your cabin, the less likely they are to break in. The burglar and vandal want to get in and out fast. The burglar needs his vehicle to haul off his loot. Deprive them of easy access.

Post your boundaries with NO TRESPASSING signs. Be firm about not wanting anybody on your property without your written permission. Most states now have strong trespassing laws, and posting your land will notify trespassers that they are not welcome. Vandals are sometimes woods roamers looking for something to burn or to destroy.

Remove any concealment such as trees, bushes, and buildings from around your cabin. The more hidden it is, the more likely it is for the lowlifes to hang around the premises. Also make it a policy to pull shades or close blinds when you leave the cabin. The less a prowler sees the less tempted he is to break in. Never leave guns or other desirables in your cabin because if the word gets out, you can bet it will be broken into.

## A WATCHFUL EYE

Get to know the local sheriff and have him or some of his chief deputies out to your cabin. Let them know that you want to be a good neighbor and would like for them to look in on your cabin. Some sheriff's departments include cabins on their patrol routes. Some local law enforcement officers will contract to check on your cabin, when they are off duty, for a reasonable fee. I have a good friend, a state conservation officer and wildlife biologist, who checks on my cabin in exchange for hunting privileges on my property. This arrangement works well for both of us.

In some areas there are companies that are in business to check remote cabins not only for burglary and vandalism, but also for other problems such as storm damage or midwinter precautions like turning on the heat to protect water pipes or shoveling off a porch roof loaded with deep snow. In northern Wisconsin in the heart of cabin country, a company called Cabin Care specializes in property management services for cabins. As more rural areas see an increase in cabins, I think we will see more companies of this type.

One of the best forms of protection is to have a local neighbor keep an eye on your cabin. They are usually on top of who is coming and going, and they are most likely know whom to watch. Also rural neighbors can check on the cabin at odd hours and know how to handle problems when they arise. A cabin I once owned in a remote area was well looked after by the nearest neighbor, who lived five miles away. There was a creek on my place he liked to fish, so we traded fishing privileges for security checks. He fell in love with the cabin and property and did a great job of looking after the place. I hated selling the cabin because I enjoyed his company.

If you have power to your cabin, consider having a light on a timer to put lights on at various hours. You may want to put in an alarm. While there may not be anyone within hearing of the alarm, it could scare the intruder off. Of course, if you have phone service you may want a more sophisticated alarm system that calls the sheriff's department.

## FOILING TROUBLEMAKERS

When you build your cabin make sure all exterior doors are solid with a long-throw deadbolt lock. Have locks on all windows. You can drill a hole, to one side, in the top of the bottom window, where it overlaps the bottom of the top window, and insert a 20-penny nail—this will slow down someone trying to force the window open.

Keep all equipment you leave at the cabin (boats, canoes, vehicles, etc.) locked in a building. Also disable any vehicles. While I was working on this book, a cabin owner near my cabin left his four-wheel-drive truck at his remote cabin. Someone walked into the cabin, hotwired the truck, and using the four-wheel drive, drove cross-country to reach a public road. Had the owner left the vehicle disabled, it might not have been taken.

Engrave any equipment and valuables you leave at your cabin with your driver's license number or some other meaningful number. Everything in my cabin has an identifying number hidden somewhere. Keep an inventory of valuables including serial numbers and model numbers.

Be sure not to help vandals by leaving axes and other tools they can use to damage or break into your cabin. Also avoid leaving flammable fluids where vandals can find them; it makes burning your cabin easy. Walk around your cabin before you leave, and think like a vandal.

## PERSONAL SAFETY

If you think your cabin has been broken into, do not go in. Get to a safe place and call law enforcement and wait until they arrive before returning. Do not disturb anything in the area. Your walking or driving around the cabin can destroy tire tracks, footprints, and other forms of evidence.

Keep the phone numbers of local law enforcement, fire departments, conservation officers, and medical services at the cabin and in your vehicle. Most areas now have 911 systems, but these other phone numbers could help. Also have the numbers of your nearest neighbors. If a cell phone works at your cabin, keep one there and charged. If not, know the location of the nearest phone.

Even when you are at the cabin, it is a good idea to keep your gate locked at night and keep your cabin door locked. Last year I was visiting friends at a remote ranch in New Mexico. The owners have a cabin in a remote part of the ranch, miles from the front gate of the ranch. The owner and his wife never locked the door of the cabin. One night the wife woke up to see two people standing over the bed. She screamed, and they ran to their truck and took off. The intruders were never caught, and no one knows who they were or why they were there. You can bet my friends now lock their cabin door.

Know and keep up to date on first aid and CPR. Remote cabins are a fun getaway, but you must be prepared for emergencies because help is further away and you may be on your own for awhile.

By following these tips and using a little common sense, you can enjoy many years of cabin fun without much risk of a serious problem.

18

---

# Managing Your Property

Throughout this book we have discussed the planning, selection, building, and use of your dream cabin but we have not discussed the land you bought or leased on which to build the cabin. Managing that land needs your faithful attention, as it will have a lot to do with your satisfaction in staying at the cabin. The two go together, so the more you do for one, the better it is for both.

We as landowners, or long-term lessees, have an obligation to be good stewards of the land and the wildlife found there. By doing a good job of managing the woodlands, wildlife, streams, ponds, and soils around your cabin site, you are assured of having a good environment to visit. Also, you become a better neighbor and protect the natural resources for future generations who will come to the cabin. Good land management is a part of good cabin management. Most cabin owners find that family and visitors alike will enjoy working on forestry or wildlife management projects. It is educational, good exercise, fun, and makes the cabin investment grow.

## PUT YOUR LAND MANAGEMENT TEAM TOGETHER

As soon as you acquire the land for your cabin, you should put a land management team together, whether you buy a one-acre lot or hundreds of acres. The nice thing about getting good land management assistance is that it is provided to you at no direct cost—you pay for it with your federal and state tax dollars.

For your basic land, soil, water, and to some extent wildlife management assistance the Natural Resource Conservation Service (NRCS) agent,

169

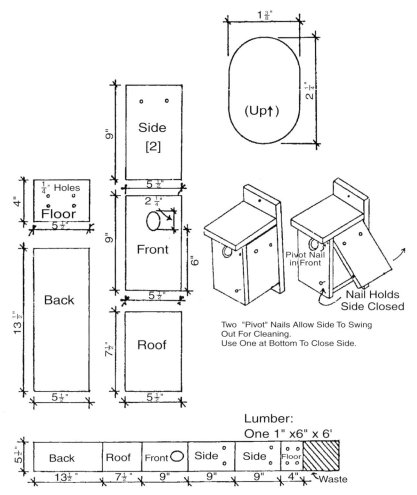

1 3/8"

2 1/4"

(Up↑)

9"

Side
[2]

5 1/2"

4"

1/4" Holes

Floor

5 1/2"

2 1/4"

9"

Front

6"

5 1/2"

Back

13 1/2"

Pivot Nail
in Front

Nail Holds
Side Closed

Two "Pivot" Nails Allow Side To Swing
Out For Cleaning.
Use One at Bottom To Close Side.

7 1/2"

Roof

5 1/2"

5 1/2"

Lumber:
One 1" x 6" x 6'

5 1/2"

| Back | Roof | Front ○ | Side ° | Side ° | Floor |  |
|------|------|---------|--------|--------|-------|--|
| 13 1/2" | 7 1/2" | 9" | 9" | 9" | 4" | Waste |

Building a bluebird house is easy, and helps improve backyard habitat.

To write a forest management plan, you must first break the property into small units called habitat types or management units. Draw them on a map. Once you know what you have, it will be easier to decide what to do with each unit. Factors to consider when determining management objectives for each unit are:

1. Uniqueness of the unit
2. Presence of unusual wildlife habitats
3. Present timber value

ing wildlife and forestry stewardship programs where you can get additional help and in some cases financial assistance. Getting to know your team members will open up many new doors for you that will make your cabin and the property it sits on more interesting and fun.

The following sections describe some of the management programs your team can help you with.

## ROAD SITING AND DEVELOPMENT

Roads are necessary on your property. They give you access to your cabin and, if the tract is large enough, to other parts of your property; however, high costs, erosion, degradation of water quality, and destruction of fish habitat can result from poor location, construction, and maintenance of roads. Today there are specific regulations for building small private roads in forest areas. Before you start laying out roads, go to your NRCS agent and county forester and have them walk your property with you to help you site roads and suggest good road maintenance practices. Also have them recommend a contractor who will get your roads developed right the first time. Ask the county agent for plans for building a gate to close your roads when they are not in use.

## LANDSCAPING AROUND THE CABIN

Once your cabin is built you may want to establish a lawn around the cabin to enhance the beauty of the site or to prevent having a muddy mess every time it rains. Regardless of the reason, your county extension agent can save you a lot of headaches and costs. Have someone from the extension office come out to the site and recommend the best plant material and how best to establish it and maintain it. They will give you a soil test kit to start with, as soil testing is a must for growing lawns, gardens, and wildlife food plots.

When planning the lawn, think about putting in a bird feeding station near a window in the cabin. Ask your county extension agent to recommend plants for your area that attract birds and butterflies. He or she can draw a cabin yard habitat plan that can turn your cabin lawn into an entertainment center for those interested in nature.

An interesting project for your cabin yard is a bluebird trail, consisting of a number of bluebird nesting boxes (see plans) spaced at least 100 yards

A well-managed lawn adds to the beauty of the cabin and helps keep mud from the interior.                                    Photo by Northeastern Log Homes

apart. Youngsters can keep logs as to which boxes were used and when the young birds left the nest. Each fall the nest boxes should be cleaned out for the next spring's use. I have a trail at my cabin, and it is of interest to everyone. For more information on bluebird trails, go to the North American Bluebird Society web site (www.nabluebirdsociety.org), and for more information on backyard wildlife habitats go to the National Wildlife Federation web site (www.nwf.org/habitats).

## MANAGING YOUR WOODLANDS

If your cabin site is in or adjacent to woodlands you own or are responsible for, then you will want to give a lot of thought to your forest management plan. Most cabin owners manage their forest for wildlife, and some for income when the timber becomes marketable.

The first step to setting up a forest management plan is to get a forester to visit your property and to help you make your management decisions. If wildlife management is a priority then you will want to get your state/district wildlife biologist to also attend the meeting. In some states the forester will write the entire plan for you once he or she knows your goals.

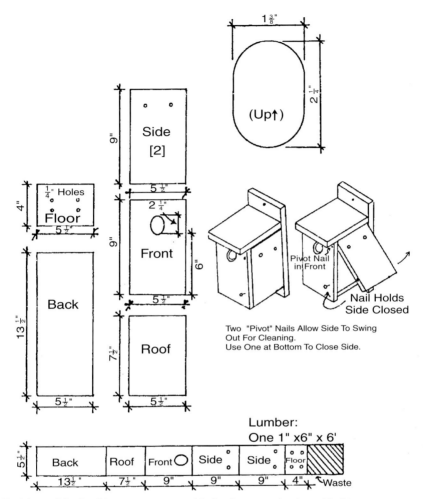

Building a bluebird house is easy, and helps improve backyard habitat.

To write a forest management plan, you must first break the property into small units called habitat types or management units. Draw them on a map. Once you know what you have, it will be easier to decide what to do with each unit. Factors to consider when determining management objectives for each unit are:

1. Uniqueness of the unit
2. Presence of unusual wildlife habitats
3. Present timber value

4. Potential for timber
5. Value for subdividing for cabin sites
6. Probable duration of ownership
7. Probable intentions or desires of future owners

Once you have established your objectives, you are ready to write your plan.

Wildfires are a danger to many cabins, and the best protection for this is to have the county forest ranger inspect your property for fire risk. He will help you plow a firebreak around the cabin and teach you how to manage it.

## WILDLIFE MANAGEMENT

Working with your local wildlife biologist to develop a wildlife management plan can be a lot of fun, particularly if you are a hunter or a nature lover. This plan will take into consideration what species of animals you wish to manage your land for and what changes you need to make to create a suitable habitat for those target species. Most often food plots will be a part of the plan, and that is where you the landowner can get involved. It gives you another reason to spend weekends at the cabin when it's time to plant the food plots.

Your state wildlife biologist will give you all the recommendations for your wildlife food plots. It will be up to you to plant them. This becomes a concern of many landowners who do not have tractors and farm equipment.

The first solution could be to have the county agent put you in contact with a local farmer who will plant the food plot for you for a small fee. A second solution, if you have an ATV, would be to use the ATV as a small tractor. Many cabin owners are learning that their ATV can be used not only for yard work but for wildlife management as well.

Mike Prechter of Metairie, Louisiana now owns one of my former cabins. He has a wildlife management program and hunts on the land surrounding the cabin. "My four-wheeler allows me to carry out the practices called for in my wildlife management plan," he says.

Having no farm equipment at the cabin property could have been a major setback in his wildlife program. But then Prechter discovered the selection of farming accessories he could attach to his ATV. "Now I enjoy wildlife management work during the 'no hunting' season as much as I do the hunting season," he says.

Like Prechter, I too have discovered the value of using an ATV to manage wildlife at my Cross Creek Hollow property. Based on my work, most

Managing wildlife food plots on a cabin property may be done by a neighboring farmer or by the cabin owner if he has a heavy-duty ATV.       Photo by JWF

four-wheel-drive ATVs of 400 cubic centimeters or more often can get the job done in areas too remote or small for farm tractors. Today there are pull behind mowers, plows, disks, and planters that will turn the ATV into a mini-tractor.

Flooding caused by beaver activity cut me off from one of my best food plots for photographing deer and wild turkeys soon after the seedbed was prepared. By hooking an electric seeder to my ATV, I got into the field to fertilize and plant it.

Other wildlife management recommendations your wildlife biologist might make could include prescribed burning of some units. The state forester can help with this. If planting mast producing trees and shrubs is a part of the plan, your team can tell you where to get these plant materials and how to manage them.

## FISHERIES MANAGEMENT

Perhaps there is a small stream on your property you would like to improve for fishing, or you have a pond or would like to build a fish pond; then you would want to add the local state fisheries biologist to your team. Managing

Stream and pond management require sound technical advice.

a stream may come under local regulations, so your fisheries biologist and NRCS agent should be consulted before you begin making any plans. If it is permissible to improve fish habitat in your stream, then a detailed plan will be designed for the target species of fish.

If a fish pond is on the property or if you want to construct one, then you should set a meeting with the fisheries biologist and NRCS agent and explore the possibilities. Building and managing fish ponds can be expensive, and they require a lot of technical know-how to do it correctly. Starting with the right team can save you a lot of money and problems.

All the land management of your cabin property should be a pleasant experience, provided you get the right help. To further its enjoyment, keep a journal as to what you do and when you do it. Also, take lots of photographs of your land management projects as they evolve, and keep them in a photo album at the cabin. Visitors will enjoy looking at your progress.

Remember your planning team when you have a cookout at the cabin. These professionals can be good friends to have in your community, and they can help make your cabin living a lot more pleasant.

CHAPTER

# Develop a Shooting Range Near Your Cabin

If you are interested in the shooting sports, then you may want to consider building a shooting range near your cabin, especially if the cabin is located in a remote area. To have a private shooting range tucked away near a cabin is the dream of many shooters. No waiting your turn, no delay in going downrange to change targets, and no audience when your daughter is learning to shoot. Here is how to develop a range on your property.

## PLANNING

Before you can begin searching for the right location on your property for the shooting range, you must have a plan for your range. This will have a lot to do with the size and location of the range site.

My family likes to shoot a variety of firearms, so when we started to build a new range we wanted to accommodate all of them. The plan we developed called for at least 3 acres of reasonably flat land for the range site. We wanted a steep hill just behind the 100-yard target stands for the impact area. The ideal site would have a downrange direction of North so that no matter what time of the day we were shooting, the sun would not be in our eyes.

We listed these requirements and others that would help ensure safety and privacy. We wanted a range site far enough from the nearest residence that the noise would not disturb neighbors.

We also wanted a buffer zone of land around the range for safety reasons, which we would post and protect from trespassers.

We didn't want our range to be situated near a public road. This was for safety, but because we wanted to store range supplies at the site, an out-of-the-way location would also help discourage break-ins and vandalism.

Our local sheriff was most helpful in making sure we followed all local ordinances and didn't inadvertently break any laws.

## LAYOUT

The layout and construction of a range are critical for safety and your satisfaction. Stake out likely positions of firing stations, target stands, pattern boards, and the like. Then review the entire range and position of the sun throughout the day. Sit on a low stool, sighting down the shooting positions to check for topographical obstacles in your line of sight. Walk through the safe zone all the way around the range to the property line and look for ways someone could wander onto the property.

Check out the range site as it relates to noise and safety. Our range is about 500 yards from our cabin, and the noise is not objectionable. The range shooting direction is safely directed away from the cabin activity.

Lay out your shooting range with safety as your primary consideration.

## DEVELOPING THE RANGE

Developing a private range near your cabin may be as simple as setting up a portable shooting bench and a target taped to a cardboard box, or as complex as reshaping the land and constructing an all-weather shooting house.

The heart of our shooting range is a 16-by-16-foot shooting house with a concrete slab floor built higher than anticipated floodwaters. The roof is made from translucent fiberglass to provide all-weather protection, yet allow plenty of light to reach the shooting bench.

Because we spend a lot of time evaluating firearms and ammunition, we wanted a heavy-duty shooting bench large enough for two, with plenty of room for a chronograph, spotting scope, and notebooks. We built a two-person bench, measuring 5 by 9 feet, from treated lumber. The six legs are set in the concrete floor.

Having previously had a shooting range with a storage room to the shooter's side, we wanted the sides of our new shooting house open to help the sound escape. We built two 4-by-8-foot rooms at the rear of the shooting house, one for storing range supplies and the second a reloading room with built in bench. Although we don't leave reloading supplies at the range, having a room set up for reloading has proven to be one of our favorite

Translucent fiberglass roof lets light in, keeps weather out.

features. It's nice to be able to test loads immediately and make changes on the spot.

Permanent chronograph stand footings are placed in front of our shooting house, so it takes only a minute or so to set up the chronograph screens.

We test lots of shotgun and loads, so we set up a pattern board range to the left side of the shooting house. It has concrete firing pads at 20, 30, 40, and 50 yards. We have a 40-by-40-inch wooden board on which to staple pattern targets.

Our 100-yard rifle target stands have 4-by-4-foot wood frames with plywood target backs. For intermediate-range shooting on the rifle range, we use a portable sign frame with a wood target back. A local service station gave us the aluminum frame.

Our pistol range, which is to the right of the shooting house, consists of a waist-high wooden pistol table constructed of two 2-by-6-inch-by-6-foot boards mounted side by side on 4-by-4-inch treated legs anchored in concrete. The metal framed, wood-backed pistol target stands are located at 7, 15, and 25 yards and are staggered so the handgunner can shoot all three from one spot.

A one-acre open area to the side of the other shooting activities is ideal for use of action targets such as Dueling Tree, swinging targets, or falling plates. It's also a good place to throw clay targets for shotgun shooting. We keep an Outers Lightning Launcher clay target thrower at the range for clay target shooting.

## STANDARD OPERATING PROCEDURES

Regardless of how few people use the small, private shooting range, there must be written operating rules that apply to everyone involved. These rules should cover safety issues, maintenance, the use of supplies and equipment, and other issues to prevent accidents and misunderstandings.

Have every visitor who uses your range sign off on these procedures and sign a liability waiver (see appendix).

It is probably easier and more affordable to develop a range near your cabin than you think, and the rewards of having a private place for your family and guests to shoot will spoil you.

The rewards of having a family shooting range are well worth the effort.

# Cabin Living

A small cabin tucked away in the woods can be one of the most pleasant possessions a person can have. The enjoyment it brings to all who spend time there cannot be measured. I know many people who live their weekly lives just thinking about the weekend at the cabin, or "camp" (as many call their getaways.)

To get the full enjoyment out of cabin living, some planning is necessary to prevent little oversights from becoming problems. Coming back to a cabin that you left a mess is no fun—you spend the first few hours working rather than getting settled in. A guest who falls off the woodpile and sues you can sour your cabin experience. Mice and insects taking over the cabin can make some people think about selling the cabin and buying a boat.

## Easy In, Easy Out

In order to have a cabin that is ever a pleasure to return to, you should always leave the cabin like it was new. At my cabin we have an exit plan. It is simple and everyone knows it, and is expected to pitch in to make it happen. Exit plans will vary with the cabin, but the principle is the same. Here is the Cross Creek Hollow departure checklist:

- All dishes are washed, dried, and put away.
- The wood-burning stove is cleaned out, ashes dumped, and reloaded so that all is takes to build a fire next time is a match. This is particularly important if you are cold and wet upon your next arrival.
- The wood and kindling box is filled.

- Beds are made or bed linens are gathered to take home for cleaning.
- Countertops and the table and oilcloth are washed and dried.
- Foodstuffs, except canned goods, are packed to take home.
- Wet wash/drying cloths are packed to take home.
- Garbage cans are emptied and cleaned out.
- Floors are swept.
- Rugs are taken out and shaken.
- The outhouse is cleaned thoroughly and fresh lime applied.
- The porch is swept.
- The cabin porch chairs are brought in.
- The cabin yard is checked for any trash.
- The windows are closed, locked, and the shades pulled.
- The door is locked.

It only takes an hour or so to close the cabin properly when you are leaving, and you will be thankful you did when you next return. Also leaving the cabin clean and orderly helps discourage mice and insects.

## BIANNUAL CLEANUPS

Since cabins get hard use in an outdoor environment, it is a good idea to have a thorough cleanup each spring and fall. We turn this into a fun weekend complete with a big cookout and if time permits a sporting clays competition (shooting clay pigeons). I invite friends that use the cabin often and there is usually a waiting list for volunteers.

Also everything in the cabin is taken outside and the cabin is given a good cleaning. We always find items that need to be taken home. The less the cabin is used as a storage building, the better and the easier it is to keep clean. During these cleanings we look for any necessary repairs and they are made then. It is a fun weekend, and the cabin benefits from the effort.

## PEST CONTROL

Keeping insect problems to a minimum is not difficult inside the cabin, even in the South. If the cabin is built tightly, stays clean, and doors are not left open for long periods of time, insects will be few. I also spray my cabin interior monthly during the warm months with a home insect control spray to give added protection. On the outside I watch during the warm months for flying/stinging insects and destroy their nests as early as possible. This has worked with all critters of that type except carpenter bees.

If you have a cabin, chances are good you will get to know carpenter bees; I call them flying beavers. Ten years ago, when I had just finished building my dream cabin, I had never had serious problems with carpenter bees. The first few years at the cabin I rarely ever saw a carpenter bee. Occasionally one would burrow a nest in an exposed rafter, but I figured that was the price of having a cabin way back in the woods; besides we need pollinators.

My understanding nature changed this past May when I arrived at the cabin to find sawdust all over the porch floor and carpenter bees, dozens of them, busy drilling holes in every exposed board they could find. At first I didn't think their boring was too serious (I guess I went fishing the day my entomology professor in college discussed carpenter bees). A little concerned, I went on the World Wide Web to see how to manage these pests. I was shocked at what I learned: their ½-inch diameter nesting tunnel can go back into a board as much as 24 inches; they return to the same nesting site each year to nest, increasing the number of bees annually; since they will use old tunnels, they increase the length of those tunnels and drill new ones. In short, buildings have been known to fall in as a result of carpenter bees having tunneled away so much of the supporting timbers that the boards broke.

All my life I had been told that carpenter bees could not sting. Wrong! The male (the one with the white head) does not, but the female can and will sting.

Armed with this knowledge and lots of information on eradication of carpenter bees, I declared war on these "flying beavers." I sprayed with the latest formulas that were supposed to stop their tunneling, but they increased their activity. I dusted their holes with recommended pesticides; a few died but I couldn't tell the difference. I plugged their holes; they ate through the plugs. The number of bees around the cabin was growing, as was the amount of sawdust.

After several weeks of the fight I was about to throw in the towel when my wife showed up with two well-made badminton racquets. I laughed it off as a joke, but when she took out the fifth bee with a nice backhand stroke, I took it seriously. That afternoon over 30 "flying beavers" were dispatched with a variety of fancy strokes, and some not so fancy. The event had the makings of a country-folks' Wimbledon, with the added adventure of female bees trying to connect with their stingers.

The bee match was a favorite pastime for the next few days and while the bees were not totally eliminated, very few survived to successfully nest.

The next time someone tells me beavers can't fly, I am going to debate that fact. If you can't get to your cabin during the warm months, especially in the South, you may want to have a contract with a professional pest control company. Buildings in remote areas that are little used can become a haven for insects.

I don't have problems with mice at my cabin; however, I still leave commercial mice bait inside when the cabin is not in use for long periods. Most cabins have mice. Using the mice baits on a regular basis can help with the problem.

## LIABILITY

This is always a touchy subject, but if you have guests visit your cabin and property, you are looking at two potential problems: someone having an accident and suing you, or their accidental destruction of your dream cabin or property through ignorance or neglect. First you will want your insurance to include liability coverage for one million dollars or more. Your insurance agent should be a part of your planning team when you start building the cabin. Many cabins give access to other potential dangers in activities like boating, fishing, hunting, mountain climbing, etc. Let your insurance agent know the details of activities in and around your cabin and make sure you are covered.

Next, consider having your guests sign a liability release. The laws in each state differ on this subject, but your attorney can advise you as to what might work where your cabin is located. A sample of the liability release I use is found in appendix 4. I think people should be responsible for their own safety, and the signing of a release helps put them on notice.

Guests need to be informed as to what is expected when using your cabin. If they are there with you, you can guide them in a friendly way, but if they are using your property and you are not around, you cannot expect them to know how to do everything. In other words, they cannot read your mind. I have found the best answer to this dilemma is to have a "standard operating procedure" (SOP) printed and to have it posted where it can be read. A copy of the SOP we use at Cross Creek Hollow is in the appendix. This document simply list the rules of the cabin and property that we expect everyone to follow. They are not to insult anyone, and I have used them for many years. I don't know of anyone who has taken exception.

When I give my permission for someone to use the cabin I usually go over the SOP with them in person or on the phone. I also have a copy in the cabin where it can be seen, and another copy is posted on the outhouse door where it stares at you when you are sitting on the "throne." I have never had a problem since I started using this document although I did have a few problems earlier.

## SPECIAL GATHERINGS

As I stated earlier, the biannual cabin cleanups are popular weekends at my cabin. You too will find occasions for special gatherings at your cabin. Bringing your family and special friends closer together, the cabin becomes the heart of everything that's most important to you. My cabin is used for grandchildren's birthdays, Thanksgiving celebration, and the Cross Creek Hollow March Mountain Man Rendezvous.

The plan for an annual weekend rendezvous was born on a hunt several years ago. A small group of friends I have been hunting with for 20-plus years were discussing the merits of having an annual camp-out where we could hold shooting competitions, try new game recipes, and sit around a campfire to relive hunts of the past. Since we all enjoyed muzzle-loading

Cabins have a special way of bringing family together.                    Photo by JWF

rifle shooting, Danny Engeron, an amateur historian from Metairie, Louisiana, came up with the idea of a mountain-man style rendezvous, reminiscent of the Rocky Mountain rendezvous of the 1830s. He suggested that we all dress in mountain-man period clothing, cook over open fires, and live like pioneers. Everyone liked the idea, and March was chosen as the month for the gathering.

The only remaining decision was where to have this event. Anthony Paternostro, a farmer from Carriere, Mississippi, suggested my cabin, since the property was ideal for target shooting and practicing a primitive lifestyle. That was 12 years ago, and this March the 12th annual Cross Creek Hollow Mountain Man Rendezvous was held.

Over the years as the group has aged, the rules have changed. Mountain-man clothing is no longer required, and we all sleep comfortably in soft bunks in the cabin rather than on the ground, but the spirit of the rendezvous is very much alive.

Early in the history of the Cross Creek Hollow Rendezvous it was decided that we would do a major wildlife management project each year in the Hollow. Of course I enjoyed this, as it was free labor to improve my property. Projects I selected each year were usually chores I could not do

Special events such as a Cross Creek Hollow Rendezvous add special meaning to owning a cabin.                                    Photo by JWF

alone, projects such as creating a wildlife opening from an old field taken over by a jungle of briers. Due to the Herculean nature of these projects, the participants now fondly refer to the Hollow as the Talladega Death Camp, named for the national forest that surrounds my property.

This year, as in years past, a feast will be prepared in Dutch ovens, reflector ovens, and the old reliable bean hole for Saturday night. A select group of invited guests will join a group of hunters who have been friends for over a quarter of a century. They will share the ageless bond of friendship around a campfire in 2002, much like the Rocky Mountain rendezvous of the 1830s. Without my cabin this special gathering may have never taken place.

## TIME ALONE

One of the most meaningful experiences you can have at your cabin is the chance to spend some time there on your own. Most of us rarely, if ever, really spend time alone. The small remote cabin is a great place to do this. Getting to know oneself is something we all need. I have spent many days alone at my cabin and I highly recommend it to anyone. You will return home a better person.

It takes several days of being alone to get into the rhythm of being totally on your own. I have found that after about the third day an inner peace comes over you as you go about your chores. Suddenly you have the time to read, and what you read you really get into. Time takes on a new meaning. You lose the rush of having to be somewhere at a particular time. You do as you need to do when on your own. It is easy to lose track of time when you spend time alone at your cabin. I guarantee that if you try it once, you will want the experience again.

## PREPARING FOR DOWNTIME

We are so accustomed to having our entertainment piped to us—television, radio, computer, telephone—that we are at a loss when there is time available. In the remote cabin many or perhaps none of these things are available. We do fine as long as the weather is good and we can go hiking, fishing, cook outside, or do outside chores. Then the day comes when it rains or snows really hard and we can't get outside. Trapped in the cabin without our electronic entertainment, what do we do?

When the weather is inclement, a small cabin with a good supply of games will not seem so small.                                                      Photo by JWF

Plan ahead for those days; they can be special also. Have games and puzzles you enjoy available. If you were to look under one of the bunk beds in my cabin now, you would find a wide spectrum of adult and children's games. Have a good selection of books you like on hand. Also, bring those magazines you never have time to read at home—now you have time. For those days that we humans are cabinbound, one of the most popular places at my cabin is in front of the window where the bird feeder is located. Here a bird identification book and binoculars are kept and they are used a lot on bad-weather days. It is better than any television.

For those who must have their electronic entertainment, there are TV sets with built-in video that can run on a deep-cycle battery. Even if you can't get TV, you can watch videos. There are radios and tape decks and CD players that run on flashlight batteries. I keep a radio in my cabin that will run for one hour after you wind it up like a clock. It is a very powerful radio with a short-wave band. I also keep a battery-operated weather radio at the cabin, not for entertainment but to keep up with the weather.

Battery-operated TVs and wind-up radios may be purchased for cabin use for those who require electronic entertainment.                    Photo by JWF

## A Cabin Name

Giving your cabin a name can be a lot of fun and it gives an identity that suits your cabin's personality, which will be with you, family, and friends from now on. Take your time, and don't settle on a name until you have one that says to you when you hear it, "My dream cabin in the woods."

# Appendix 1

## Sources

### CABIN CONSTRUCTION

**Adirondack Shelter Plans**
*A Guide to Log Lean-to Construction*
Maine Appalachian Trail Club
Box 283
Augusta, Maine 04330

**Self-sufficient Cabin Equipment Catalogs**
Cumberland General Store
#1 Hwy 68
Crossville, TN 38555
800–334–4640
**www.cumberlandgeneral.com**

Lehman's
P. O. Box 41
Kidron, OH 44636
330–857–5757
**www.lehmans.com**

**Cabin Exterior Protection**
Olympic
PPG Architectural Finishes Inc.
One PPG Place
Pittsburg, PA 15272
**www.olympic.com**

Perma-Chink
1605 Prosser Road
Knoxville, TN 37914
Tennessee 800–548–3554
Colorado 800–433–8781
Minnesota 877–244–6548
Montana 800–479–7090
Washington 800–548–1231
**www.permachink.com**

Sash Co.
10300 E. 107th Pl.
Brighton, CO 80601
800–767–5656
**www.sashco.com**

Weatherall Co.
106 Industrial Way
Charlestown, IN 47111
800–367–7068
**www.weatherall.com**

## Log Siding

Anthony Log Homes
P. O. Box 1877
El Dorado, Arkansas 71731
800–837–8786
**www.anthonyforest.com**

Logsiding.Com
Designs by DSD
HCR 3 Box 3699 Pennaxing
Lewiston, MI 49756
989–786–5089
**www.logsiding.com**

Glu-Lam-log, Inc.
2872 Hwy 93 N.
Victor, MT 59875
406–777–3219
**www.glulamlog.com**

EZ Home Kits
2820 Audubon Village Dr. #186
Audubon, PA 19403
877–355–7510
**www.ezhomekits.com**

Great Southern Log Homes
P. O. Box 576
Picayune, MS 39466
601–798–8129

T. R. Miller Mill Co.
P. O. Box 708
Brewton, AL 36427
334–867–4331

## Log Cabin Kits

Appalachian Log Homes, Inc.
11312 Station West Drive
Knoxville, TN 37922
800–726–0708
**www.alhloghomes.com**

Heritage Log Homes, Inc.
P.O. Box 8080
Sevierville, TN 37864
800–456–4663
**www.heritagelog.com**

Honest Abe Log Homes, Inc.
3855 Clay County Highway
Moss, TN 38575
800–231–3695
**www.honestabe.com**

Jim Barna Log Systems
P.O. Box 4529
Oneida, TN 37841–4529
Phone: 423–569–5903, 800–962–4734
**www.logcabins.com**

Northeastern Log Homes, Inc./ VERMONT
P.O. Box 126
Groton, VT 05046–0126
800–992–6526

Northeastern Log Homes/MAINE
P.O. Box 46
Kenduskeag, ME 04450–0046
800–624–2797

Northeastern Log Homes/MASSACHUSETTS
1126 Southampton Rd.
Westfield, MA 01085–1368
800–528–4456

Northeastern Log Homes/KENTUCKY
P.O. Box 7966
Louisville, KY 40257–0966
800–451–2724
**www.northeasternlog.com**

The Wilderness Cabin Co.
415 Neave Court
Kelowna, BC Canada V1V 2M2
888–891–3111, 250–765–0535
**www.wildernesscabin.com**

Suwannee River Log Homes
4345 U.S. 90
Wellborn, FL 32094
**www.srloghomes.com**

Tennessee Log Homes
2537 Decatur Pike
Athens, TN 37303
800–251–9218, 423–744–8156
**www.tnloghomes.com**

Kuhns Brothers Log Homes
Lewisburg, PA
800–326–9614
**www.kuhnsbros.com**

Panel Concepts, Inc.
331 No. M-33
Mio, MI 48647
989–826–6511
**www.panelconcepts.com**

Ward Log Homes
P.O. Box 72
Houlton, ME 04730
800–341–1566
**www.wardloghomes.com**

## BOOKS

### Books on Building Cabins

Most of these books can be found at:
 **www.amazon.com**
 **www.alibris.com**
 **www.lyonspress.com**
 **www.barnesandnoble.com**

Log Cabins and How to Build Them, by William Swanson, The
 Lyons Press
Building the Alaska Log Home, by Tom Walker, Alaska Northwest
 Books
Living Homes, by Thomas J. Elpels, HOPS Press ( www.hollowtop.com)

Back to Basics, Readers Digest

Complete Guide to Building Log Homes, by Monte Burch, Stackpole Books

The Wilderness Cabin, by Calvin Rutstrum, Collier Books

Cabin Fever: Sheds and Shelters, Huts and Hideaways, by Marie France Boyer

Rustic Retreats: A Build-It-Yourself Guide, by D. R. Stiles and J. T. Stiles

Small Log Homes, by Robbin Obomsawin

Shelters, Shacks and Shanties and How to Build Them, by D.C. Beard, The Lyons Press

## Books on Cabin Living

Cache Lake Country, by John Rowlands, The Countryman Press

One Man's Wilderness, by Sam Keith, Alaska Northwest Books

The Cheechakoes, by Wayne Short, Random House

At Home in the Woods, by Vena and Bradford Angier, Sheridan House

## Books on Buying Raw Land

Buying & Selling Country Land, by Daniel Reisman

Buying Country Property, by Irvin Price, Pyramid Books

Country Property Dirt Cheap, by R. C. Turner, Legalis Publishing Co.

Country Acres, by L. L. Klessig, Diane Publishing Co.

Moving to the Country, by Don Skillman, Stackpole Books

## Outhouse Newsletter

The Outhouse Preservation Society
P.O. Box 25065
Halifax, NS B3M 4H4
Canada

## Seat for Outhouse

Zeebest, Inc.
11941 121 St.
Edmonton, AB T5L 4H7
Canada
780–447–5222 (Canada) 866–933–2378
**www.zeebest.com**

## Composting Toilet

Sancor
140–30 Milner Ave.
Scarborough, ON
Canada M1S 3R3
800–387–5126 (USA)
**www.envirolet.com**

## Water Supply—Water Filters

PUR Water Purification Products
9300 N. 75th Ave.
Minneapolis, MN 55428
763–315–5500
**www.purwater.com**

Katadyn
1721 N Texas
Odessa, TX 79761
800–760–7942
**www.katadyn.net**

## Water Pumps

Honda Power Equipment Group
4900 Marconi Drive
Alpharetta, GA 30005

Kawasaki
**www.kawasaki.com**

## Fire Ring

Pilot Rock Park Equipment
R. J. Manufacturing Company
P.O. Box 946
Cherokee, IA 51012
800–762–5002
**www.pilotrock.com**

## Dutch Ovens

Lodge Manfacturing Corp.
P. O. Box 380
South Pittsburg, TN 37380
**www.lodgemfg.com**

## Dutch Oven Recipes

International Dutch Oven Society
41 E. 400 North #210
Logan, UT 84321
**www.idos.com**

## Reflector Ovens and Cabin Stoves

Sims Stoves
P. O. Box 21405
Billings, MT 59104
**www.wtp.net/simsstov**

Campmor
P.O. Box 700-K
Saddle River, NJ 07458
**www.campmor.com**

Fox Hill Corp.
P.O. Box 259
Rozet, WY 85727
**www.foxhill.net**

The Coleman Company
3600 North Hydraulic
Wichita, KS 67219
316–832–2653
**www.coleman.com**

# Cabin Lighting and Utilities

## Lanterns, Coolers, Heaters
The Coleman Company
3600 North Hydraulic
Wichita, KS 67219
316–832–2653
www.coleman.com

American Camper
6501 E. Apache
Tulsa, OK 74115
800–255–6061

## Generators
Coleman Powermate
P.O. Box 6001
Kearney, NE 68848
www.colemanpowermate.com

Sears Craftsman
(Local Sears store)
800–349–4358
www.sears.com

Honda Power Equipment Group
4900 Marconi Dr.
Alpharetta, GA 30005
800–426–7701
www.hondapowerequipment.com

## Generator Load Center
Gen/Tran Corp.
P.O. Box 1001
Alpharetta, GA 30004
770–552–1417
www.gen-tran.com

## Cabin Security

Cabin-Care
1470 Silver Lake Rd.
Eagle River, WI 54521
**www.cabin-care.com**

# Appendix 2

## Chain Saw Safety

### FUELING AND STARTING THE SAW

Make sure that your saw is in top operating condition; follow the manufacturer's recommendations for service and maintenance. Keep the chain properly sharpened. Maintain proper chain tension; carefully observe it, especially during the first half-hour of cutting. The lower chain span should just touch to bottom bar rails. Raise up on the bar tip while tightening the bar fasteners.

Good fire safety practices are necessary when refueling the chain saw. Refuel the saw in an open area after it has cooled, at least 10 feet away from where you wish to restart the saw and resume cutting. Fuel the saw at least 20 feet away from fires and cigarettes. Use proper funnels and spouts to prevent spills. Wipe the saw dry of any spilled fuel before cranking it.

Place the saw on a clear, firm, flat surface as close to the work area as possible. Get a good footing. Follow the owner's manual recommendations for starting the chain saw. Place your foot in the handle to restrain the saw if designed with this intention. Never start the saw on your knee; too many experienced woodsmen have slipped and cut their legs.

### FELLING THE TREE

Plan a safe approach to cutting the tree. Size up the tree, noting the wind direction and the way it is leaning. If the tree is leaning, try it in that direction when the wind is not blowing against it. If you are inexperienced, try to fell only trees that will fall in a predictable, safe direction.

Examine trees for loose, dead limbs before felling. Loose limbs that fall onto the tree cutter are a common cause of serious injuries and fatalities. Either remove the limb first, or fell the tree from a position where the limb could not strike you if it was dislodged.

Clear a safe work area around the base of the tree. Remove low limbs, underbrush and other obstructions. Be sure to have several open pathways away from the tree for an escape route when the tree begins to fall.

Be sure that clearance in the intended direction is adequate for the tree to fall completely to the ground. A lodged tree is very dangerous. Trees that hang up or snag in adjacent trees often kill experienced loggers. A tree springing back from the weight of a falling tree can whip a broken limb toward the cutter with tremendous speed.

After determining the direction of fall and clearing escape routes, cut the tree as follows:

Make one cut through for trees that measure less than 8 inches in diameter.

For larger trees, notch (undercut) at least one-third of the trunk diameter on the fall side of the trunk. Make the lower cut of the notch first to prevent the loose wedge of wood from pinching or bending the chain.

Make a felling or back cut on the opposite side of the trunk 2 inches above and parallel to the horizontal cut in the notch. The tree should begin to fall when you are several inches from the inner face of the notch. Leave a narrow uncut portion to serve as a hinge for controlling the fall of the tree.

If the saw begins to bind in a closing cut, you may have misjudged it. At the very first indication of binding, remove the saw. If it is too late to remove the saw, do not struggle with it. Shut off the engine, and plan a way to remove the saw using wedges.

Wedges are the most dependable way of controlling the direction a tree falls. Using two wedges rather than one is best. Two wedges allow better control and ensure a forward fall of the tree.

The path of the butt of a falling tree is unpredictable. Being struck by the butt, rebounding limbs, or broken tops is the second most common cause of death to those felling timber.

Controlling tree fall comes with experience. Get advice and help from an experienced person before attempting a difficult fall. Remember, accident statistics show that overconfidence can hurt experienced loggers. It may lead to dangerous shortcuts, such as not providing clear escape routes from a falling tree. Or it may lead to attempting too much, dulling the senses to danger signals.

## LIMBING THE TREE

The next job is to remove the limbs. Be alert for flexible limbs that can wedge and whip a chain saw, and avoid cluttered work areas. Serious injuries may occur during the limbing operation. Heed the following safety tips:

Begin limbing at the base of the trunk. The first limbs cut should be those on top of the trunk. Cut these as far up the side of the trunk as possible before removing those resting on the ground.

Stand on the opposite side of the trunk from the limb being cut. The trunk provides a barrier between you and the saw and helps protect you from accidental contact with the chain.

Do not hold a running saw with one hand and clear limbs with the other. Shut off the saw and put it down until limbs have been cleared.

Cutting bottom branches resting on the ground may be necessary to clear the area as you work. Beware that the tree may sag or roll as a new branch is cut. The likelihood of the tree rolling increases as more branches are removed. Be alert for any trunk movement, and be ready to move away quickly if necessary.

## BUCKING THE LOGS

Bucking is cutting the trunk of the felled tree into desired lengths. The greatest hazards while bucking a tree are unexpected log roll and saw kickback. Here are a few safety tips.

Always be sure of your footing. By keeping yourself in a well-balanced position at all times, you can react to unexpected log movement.

Raise and chock the trunk when possible to prevent rolling. Work on the uphill side of the log. Since a log rolls downhill, working on the uphill side provides the greater safety.

Bucking procedures differ depending on how you support the log. When the log is flat on the ground, cut it from the top, then roll it over and cut it through from the opposite side. When the log is supported on one end, cut one-third of the diameter from the underside to avoid pinching and splintering, then cut the remaining two-thirds of the diameter from the top. On a log supported at both ends, make the first cut through the top one-third of the diameter. Then cut the remaining wood upward from the bottom.

When cutting firewood lengths, several methods can be used. One way is to make cuts about three-fourths of the way through for each length of firewood. By not cutting completely through, several lengths stay together and the log remains rigid. After all cuts are made from one side, roll the log over and complete the cuts. Avoid sawing into the ground, which dulls the chain and shortens its useful life.

## SPLITTING THE WOOD

Splitting wood is a skill that improves with experience. Having the proper tools makes the job easier. Tools used to split firewood include a splitting ax, a sledgehammer, a splitting maul, and wedges.

The quickest way to split small, easy-to-split pieces is with an ax. An ax can get stuck, however, in larger pieces. A splitting maul makes the job easier. This tool is a combination of an ax and a maul, but with a built-in wedge on one side of the head and a hammer on the other. Use the wedge side just as you would an ax; the broader wedge keeps the blade from jamming as easily in wood. With stubborn pieces, the hammer side can be used to pound the occasional wedge. You may need a sledgehammer and wedges for larger pieces that are very hard to split.

Felling trees, cutting firewood, and operating a chain saw have a high risk of injury. Anyone near these activities should be alert to the hazards and communicate their intentions. Use a sharp chain saw, follow safe practices, maintain clear escape routes, and plan ahead to work safely and profitably.

# Appendix 3

## Ratings for Cabin Firewood

| SPECIES | RELATIVE AMOUNT OF HEAT | BURN EASY | SPLIT EASY | HEAVY SMOKE | RATING |
|---------|-------------------------|-----------|------------|-------------|--------|
| **Hardwoods** | | | | | |
| Ash | high | yes | yes | no | excellent |
| Red oak | high | yes | yes | no | excellent |
| White oak | high | yes | yes | no | excellent |
| Beech | high | yes | yes | no | excellent |
| Hickory | high | yes | yes | no | excellent |
| Hard maple | high | yes | yes | no | excellent |
| Pecan | high | yes | yes | no | excellent |
| Dogwood | high | yes | yes | no | excellent |
| Walnut | medium | yes | yes | no | good |
| Soft maple | medium | yes | yes | no | good |
| Cherry | medium | yes | yes | no | good |
| Elm | medium | medium | no | medium | fair |
| Gum | medium | medium | no | medium | fair |
| Sycamore | medium | medium | no | medium | fair |
| Aspen | low | yes | yes | medium | fair |
| Basswood | low | yes | yes | medium | fair |
| Cottonwood | low | yes | yes | medium | fair |
| Yellow poplar | low | yes | yes | medium | fair |

## Softwoods

| | | | | | |
|---|---|---|---|---|---|
| Southern yellow pine | high | yes | yes | yes | good |
| Douglas fir | high | yes | yes | yes | good |
| Cypress | medium | medium | yes | medium | fair |
| Redwood | medium | medium | yes | medium | fair |
| White cedar | medium | yes | yes | medium | good |
| Western red cedar | medium | yes | yes | medium | good |
| Eastern red cedar | medium | yes | yes | medium | fair |
| White pine | low | medium | yes | medium | fair |
| Sugar pine | low | medium | yes | medium | fair |
| Ponderosa pine | low | medium | yes | medium | fair |
| Firs | low | medium | yes | medium | fair |
| Tamarack | medium | yes | yes | medium | fair |
| Larch | medium | yes | yes | medium | fair |
| Spruce | low | yes | yes | medium | poor |

# Appendix 4

## Liability Release Form

### RELEASE OF LIABILITY AND ACKNOWLEDGMENT OF DANGERS, RISKS, AND HAZARDS OF HUNTING OR VISITING ON CROSS CREEK HOLLOW FARM, 591 COUNTY ROAD 66, HEFLIN, AL 36264

This is my acknowledgment that this document is sufficient warning that natural and man-made dangerous conditions, risks, and hazards do exist on this property. My presence and activities on the premises expose me and my property to dangerous conditions, risks, and hazards, including but not limited to the following: elevated hunting stands, whether or not erected by the landowners; shooting activities; poisonous snakes, insects, and spiders; use of all-terrain vehicles and tractors; use of target throwing equipment; hazardous and dangerous driving and walking conditions; animals both wild and domesticated that may be potentially dangerous; deep and/or swift water; persons with firearms both on or off the premises; and the use of vehicles. I hereby state that I expressly assume all such dangers, risks, and hazards.

In consideration for the rights to enter the premises, I hereby release and agree to protect, indemnify, and hold harmless the landowners and their respective agents, employees, employers, and assigns from and against any and all claims, demands, causes of action, and damages, including attorneys' fees, resulting from any accident, incident, or occurrence arising out of, incidental to, or in any way resulting from the use of the premises and improvements thereon, whether or not caused by the landowners' negligence or gross negligence. This release applies during the time that I am permitted on the premises. I hereby further covenant and agree that my heirs, my successors, assigns, and I will not make any claim or institute any suit or action at law or in equity against the landowners or their respective heirs, agents, representatives, employees, successors, or assigns.

As used in this release, the terms *I, my person,* and *myself* include minors in my care while on the premises.

Dated and signed this_____ day

of _____, 20_____

_____          _____
(Signature)                        (Printed Name)

                                   _____
                                   Address:

# Appendix 5

## Cross Creek Hollow
## Standard Operating Procedure

1. Keep vehicle use to a minimum to prevent damage to roads and fields.
2. Vehicles should not be taken inside cabin fence unless absolutely necessary.
3. Remember that clay target throwers can be extremely dangerous. Only responsible adults should use target throwers or be inside target thrower houses: absolutely no children are allowed inside houses for any reason. Bring your own clay targets.
4. Ear and eye protection are required of both shooters and spectators for all shooting activities.
5. No target practice is to be done on the property except on designated ranges.
6. Shotgun pattern boards are for shotguns firing lead shot only. No rifles, pistols, or steel shot may be used.
7. On rifle, pistol, and pattern board ranges, only one shooter at a time should be on the firing line. All other firearms should be left in the rack unloaded.
8. No breakable objects such as soft drink bottles are to be used as targets.
9. On the sporting clays course, only one position is to be used at a time, and only one shooter at a time should be in shooting position. All other shooters should have shotguns unloaded and actions open.

10. All state and federal game laws must be obeyed. All special hunting regulations imposed by owners must be obeyed.
11. Absolutely no hunting or fishing by anyone without permission.
12. Keep all gates closed and locked at all times, unless the owner states differently.
13. *No smoking* inside cabin. If you must smoke outside, do not throw cigarette butts on ground.
14. Never leave the front of the stove open without the fire screen in place. Do not leave the cabin with front of stove open, even with fire screen.
15. Never use any flammable fuel as a fire starter.
16. Never fill the stove with lighter wood; use only a few pieces to start a fire, and then add split firewood. Filling the stove with lighter wood will cause intense heat and a result in cabin fire.
17. Never burn trash in the stove.
18. If using the generator, be sure to check the oil level with each use.
19. After using the cook stove, make sure the burners are turned *off.*
20. Do not set hot pots and pans on countertops or table without pads.
21. Do not put anything but human waste and toilet paper in the outhouse pit. Toilet paper rolls, sanitary napkins, cigarette butts, and garbage of any kind goes into the cabin trash.
22. Use lime in the outhouse—every time.
23. Upon leaving the outhouse, leave the toilet seat down.
24. Chairs are not to be left on the porch.
25. Do not cut trees, bushes, flowers, etc. without permission.
26. Any problems or suspected problems should be reported to the owners promptly.
27. No guests except those invited by owners.
28. To be a guest and use the Hollow, you must sign a liability release form.
29. Bring your own sleeping bag or sheets and blankets, towels, etc.
30. Deer harvest:
    Only one buck per guest per year, and it must be eight points or better with a spread outside the ears. If you will not have it mounted, do not shoot it.
31. To hunt doe deer, you must have a DMP tag.
32. Data must be taken from bucks and does per the DMP Program.

# Appendix 6

## Cross Creek Hollow Departure Checklist

1. Make sure all shooting ranges are clean and range/sporting clays houses left clean and neat. All brass, including .22 rim fire cases and shot shell hulls should be removed. Used targets should be taken down and carried out with garbage.
2. Replace anything you use: firewood, kindling, propane, kerosene, Coleman fuel, gasoline, food, drinks, water, etc. Leave the wood box and kindling baskets full.
3. Remove ashes from stove and clean up the mess made emptying ashes. Leave stove ready to light.
4. Refill the lanterns with appropriate fuel.
5. Collect garbage from cabin, woodshed, and shooting range and re-place garbage bags. Take the garbage out with you.
6. Wipe the table and countertops clean.
7. Sweep cabin floor, porch, outhouse, and bench area of range house thoroughly.
8. Bring the porch chairs inside.
9. Leave the dishes clean and put away.
10. Hang the wet dishtowels so they can dry.
11. Close and lock the cabin windows and pull shades.
12. Make sure the range equipment is put away and covers are on the sporting clays machines.
13. Range house doors should be closed with snaps in place.
    All perishable foods should be taken out, and any non-perishable foods that are leftover should be sealed tightly.
14. Make sure all doors and gates are left locked.

15. If you eat it, drink it, burn it, break it, or use it, replace it. If you get it dirty, clean it.

Cross Creek Hollow was bought and the facilities built for our own use, personal and professional. All invitations extended to others for their use should be seen as an act of friendship. However, we will not accept responsibility for the actions, accidents, illnesses, or failures of others. If you are not willing to accept full responsibility for yourself while on these premises, please do not accept our invitation.

# Appendix 7

## Soil Testing the Cabin Yard, Wildlife Food Plot, or Garden

To have an attractive lawn around your cabin, or a healthy wildlife food plot or vegetable garden near your cabin, you will want to take a soil test. The results of this test will tell you how to fertilize and lime the ground for proper balance of nutrients and optimum soil pH level. Time and money are saved when you apply only the fertilizer needed. Over-fertilization may cause harm to plant materials and contimate your ground-water.

1. Go to your local county agent's office (Cooperative Extension Service) and get a soil test kit. It will consist of soil sample bags, information sheets, and shipping box. Do-it-yourself soil test kits may be purchased from garden supply stores also.
2. Get the tools you will need to take the samples—a clean bucket and a clean garden trowel, spade, or soil probe.
3. Following the information given in the soil test kit directions select several sites to take samples.
4. At each test site in the yard or field, scrape off any plant material from the soil surface. Push the trowel into the soil 3 to 4 inches deep.
5. Discard the soil and cut a one-inch slice from the back of the hole. Place a slice in the bucket. Do this at each test site.
6. Throughly mix the slices and pour them into the sample bag.
7. Fill out the bag with the requested information.
8. Send bag to the state testing lab listed in the kit instructions. A small fee is usually charged.
9. You will receive the test results with recommendations as to amounts and types of fertilizer, and lime needed for your intended crop.

# Appendix 8

## Average Wattage Requirement Guide

| Cabin Use | Running Wattage Requirements | Additional Wattage Required For Starting |
|---|---|---|
| Coffee Maker | 1750 | 0 |
| Dishwasher (Cool Dry) | 700 | 1400 |
| Electric Fry Pan | 1300 | 0 |
| Electric Range 8" Element | 2100 | 0 |
| Microwave Oven 625 watts | 625 | 800 |
| Refrigerator or Freezer | 700 | 2200 |
| Automatic Washer | 1150 | 2300 |
| Electric Clothes Dryer | 5750 | 1800 |
| Lights | as indicated on bulb | 0 |
| Radio | 50 to 200 | 0 |
| Television—Color | 300 | 0 |
| Central Air Conditioner— 10,000 BTUs | 1500 | 2200 |
| **Portable Heater (Kerosene, diesel fuel)** | | |
| 50,000 BTUs | 400 | 600 |
| 90,000 BTUs | 500 | 725 |
| 150,000 BTUs | 625 | 1000 |
| **Computers** | | |
| Desktop | 600 to 800 | 0 |
| Laptop | 200 to 250 | 0 |
| Monitor | 200 to 250 | 0 |
| Fax | 600 to 800 | 0 |
| Copier | 400 to 600 | 0 |

# Index